Motorsport's Military Heroes

Motorsport's Military Heroes

Iconic individuals and their stories of bravery in conflict and racing

Bryan Lightbody

Pen & Sword
MILITARY
AN IMPRINT OF PEN & SWORD BOOKS LTD.
YORKSHIRE - PHILADELPHIA

First published in Great Britain in 2022 by
Pen and Sword Transport
An imprint of
Pen & Sword Books Ltd.
Yorkshire - Philadelphia

ISBN 9781399097116

Typeset in INDIA By IMPEC eSolutions
Printed and bound in England by CPI Group (UK) Ltd, Croydon CR0 4YY.

Pen & Sword Books Ltd incorporates the imprints of Pen & Sword Books
Archaeology, Atlas, Aviation, Battleground, Discovery, Family History, History,
Maritime, Military, Naval, Politics, Railways, Select, Transport, True Crime,
Fiction, Frontline Books, Leo Cooper, Praetorian Press, Seaforth Publishing,
Wharncliffe and White Owl.

For a complete list of Pen & Sword titles please contact

PEN & SWORD BOOKS LIMITED
47 Church Street, Barnsley, South Yorkshire, S70 2AS, England
E-mail: enquiries@pen-and-sword.co.uk
Website: www.pen-and-sword.co.uk

or

PEN AND SWORD BOOKS
1950 Lawrence Rd, Havertown, PA 19083, USA
E-mail: Uspen-and-sword@casematepublishers.com
Website: www.penandswordbooks.com

Contents

Bryan Lightbody has been an army reservist, he has worked for MI5, and he has been a policeman. In the last twelve years of his police career he worked in royalty mobile and close protection, tasked with the safety of senior members of the British royal family, serving with Her Majesty the Queen in the UK and abroad. He also spent seven years as a police advanced car and motorcycle instructor. It was a dream job for a 'petrolhead' and complemented his interest in motorsport. In 2000 and 2001 he rode a motorcycle in the International Police Road Rally, a public road race in Liège, Belgium. He is a member of the Goodwood Road Racing Club. He has written three historical novels, specialising in plots of which he has a professional knowledge. He also works as a First World War battlefield guide, and a security advisor in matters of personal close protection. He lives mostly in Norfolk and France, but his consulting role takes him worldwide.

Introduction & Acknowledgements

I am fortunate to have inherited the 'petrolhead' gene from my late father, and a passion for history probably from my late maternal uncle. I acquired an interest in the military from my older brother and from my time as an army reservist. As a policeman, I spent most of my time in active driving duties in Traffic Patrol, as an instructor at the Metropolitan Police Driving School, and as a member of the Special Escort Group. In my role as a close protection officer I was frequently involved in specialist vehicle movements in a variety of covert cars and motorcycles. These were all exciting jobs.

Away from work I have had a passion for watching motorsport live, on the television, taking part in motorsport events and owning cars and motorcycles to drive, ride, cherish and preserve. All of these factors drew me to the events held at Goodwood House and circuit and eventual membership of the GRRC. My passion for classic cars led me to appear in season one of Yesterday TV Channel's 'Bangers & Cash' with my Rover SD1.

Then there was a 'lightbulb' moment when I realised that I could combine my interest in military history with my interest in motorsports. Those connections I have attempted to document in this book. I hope you enjoy the narratives as much as I did discovering and presenting them.

For their advice, assistance or support in this project I'd like to express my gratitude to my partner Sharron Rushbrook, battlefield guides and historians Mark & Mary Banning, writer and militaria expert Martin Pegler, writer and founder of 'For the Love of Books' Sarah Banham, battlefield guides Eugenie Brooks and Brian Shaw, Lee Richards at Arcre Research, Simon and Cath Kidston, Gail Woolston, and the subjects of the book for inspiring me to tell their stories. Most of the illustrations are from public domain sources, either with no copyright indication or they are over sixty years old. I have made efforts to establish issues of copyright to the best of my abilities, and if there has been an omission please get in touch.

I would particularly like to dedicate this book to Murray Walker OBE as he passed away as I completed this very personal project.

Chapter 1

Captain Woolf Barnato (1895-1948)

Royal Field Artillery in the First World War

Wing Commander RAF in the Second World War

Three times Le Mans winner & Bentley Boy

Joel Woolf Barnato, born 27 September 1895, was a British financier and racing driver, and became one of the famous 'Bentley Boys' of the 1920s. He achieved three consecutive wins out of three entries in the 24 Hours of Le Mans race. He was also a veteran of both world wars.

He was the youngest son of Fanny Bees and Barney Barnato, who made a fortune as a 'Randlord' (the term coined for entrepreneurs who controlled gold and diamond mining) in South Africa.

Barney was not born into wealth and privilege, but into the slums of Whitechapel, East London, 26 years before 'Jack the Ripper' would terrorise the population in autumn 1888.

Woolf's father's life was as remarkable as his own. Barnet Isaacs was the son of a second-hand clothes trader, but young Barnet wanted more from life than being in the 'rag trade', then and still synonymous with Whitechapel. Barney was stage-struck as a youth, perhaps from the local Wilton's music hall. He would try to cadge theatre tickets from those leaving a performance early to sell them to those arriving late, so he knew how to make a quick buck. Barney was strong and dexterous (traits that Woolf inherited). He trained to be a juggler and took up boxing. He also tried some acting, which was when he changed his name to Barney.

In the early 1870s his elder brother left for South Africa in search of gold and diamonds. Keen to find his fortune Barney followed him, it is said with between £25 and £50 and a box of cigars. Shrewd, physically tough, ambitious but lacking social polish, he grafted and flourished, then along with his brothers opened the offices of Barnato Brothers in 1874, expanding into London in 1880. In 1888 De Beers Consolidated Mines was formed, with Barney and Cecil Rhodes as life governors.

Having accumulated wealth, he spent in a carefree way – though some might have described it as vulgar. He took up with Frances Christina 'Fanny' Bees, and when she fell pregnant in 1892 they married. They went on to have three children, of whom Woolf 'Babe' Barnato was the youngest.

Woolf was born at Spencer House, 27 St James's Place, London, a stone's throw from the seats of British Royalty at Clarence House and Buckingham Palace. He had a sister, Leah Primrose, who died in 1933, and a brother, Isaac 'Jack' Henry, who died in 1918 of bronchial pneumonia, possibly linked to the Spanish flu epidemic. The family divided their time between London, Brighton, Colwyn Bay and South Africa.

In 1897, when Woolf was two years old, his father died near Madeira during a sea crossing from South Africa to London. The official verdict was suicide – death by drowning while temporarily insane. Barney had spent nine years suffering with depression and alcoholism after the collapse of a bank he founded in 1887. He lost interest in his appearance, struggled to sleep, developed paranoid thoughts about the world around him, and in June 1897 threw himself from the deck of a ship.

Woolf inherited his father's fortune, but with the monies placed in trust. He realised the first instalment of £250,000 in 1914 at the age of 19. In addition, Woolf benefited from a further inheritance after the murder of his paternal (his father's sister's son) cousin Woolf Barnato-Joel in Johannesburg in 1898. It has been speculated that Soloman 'Solly' Barnato-Joel murdered Barney as they were on deck together on RMS *Scot* when Barney apparently jumped overboard, but nothing has been proved.

Barney's funeral was as epic as his 45 years of life. Two hundred carriages followed his coffin on its way to his burial in Willesden in June 1897; but it is unlikely that Woolf would have had any recollection of it at 2 years of age.

Woolf Barnato was given the nickname 'Babe', which was either a reference to his position as the third and last of the children, or an ironic reference to his stocky six-foot frame. He was educated at Charterhouse and then Trinity College, Cambridge, where he made a name for himself as a boxer; he was renowned for flooring the heaviest of boxing 'blues'. He was a tremendous all-round athlete. He became noted as 'one of the all-time greatest athletes of his generation'.

After Charterhouse, at university, along with his brother he joined the Officer Training Corps. When the Great War broke out in 1914 he enlisted as a second lieutenant, going on to become a captain and serving in France, Egypt and Palestine in the Royal Field Artillery of the British Army. His brother Jack was a pilot in the war, involved in the bombing of Constantinople, and was mentioned in dispatches before his death from pneumonia in 1918.

Woolf packed up and left Trinity two months after war had been declared. Details are vague, but it seems that he attended an initial training camp just outside London, where he became aware of how unprepared the UK was for war, with a lack of uniforms and only one rifle for every three men. With his OTC experience he was required to coach fellow recruits. At Aldershot, to where he moved next, equipment was also in short supply.

His period in training gave him the opportunity to play team sports and hone his sporting prowess. He saw Christmas 1914 in at home before returning to the army to train in artillery. In April 1915 he was learning to fire large artillery pieces on Salisbury Plain.

He received his deployment notification in the summer of 1915, and with his brigade (the XC 90th light division) assigned to the British Army's 20th Division. Woolf's brigade comprised numbers 280, 281 and 282 Batteries RFA and the Brigade Ammunition Column. It was placed under command of the 20th (Light) Division. The brigade remained with the division until late August 1916 when it was broken up.

They shipped out to the front line in France in July 1915, being deployed close to Saint Omer. Both belligerents were dug into static trench warfare. Woolf's batteries were equipped with eighteen-pound artillery guns with a range of three to four miles, so they were dug in well behind the front lines. Those batteries equipped with shorter-range howitzers were closer to the front. Eventually his unit moved to near the French/Belgian border in the vicinity of Fleurbaix, close to Fromelles, where Australian and British infantry battalions would suffer heavy casualties the following year.

Two thirds of casualties in the First World War were as a result of artillery action, often men literally being vaporised, or their bodies pulverised or dismembered, hence the huge number of 'unknown soldier' graves, and several memorials dedicated to the hundreds of thousands of missing men. Woolf would have lived amongst this daily horror.

In February 1916 Woolf's brigade was moved into Belgium to support the defence of the Ypres Salient, where the brief was to defend Ypres at all costs. Barnato's division was supporting Canadian infantry defending hilltops around the salient at Hill 62 (Tor Top), Mount Sorrel and Hill 61. This defence involved a counterattack to regain ground lost during the summer. Barnato's unit was providing the support for this action.

After the Battle of Mount Sorrel the XC 90th Light Division was transferred back to France and the region of the Somme to act in support of the impending 'Big Push' of 1 July 1916. What was supposed to break the German line in a day lasted until 18 November, and on the first day alone had cost the lives of 19,240 British soldiers. In August the RFA XC Brigade was broken up and reassigned to larger divisions. Barnato's battery was transferred to IX Corps of the Egyptian Expeditionary Force.

By the autumn of 1916 Barnato had settled into his EEF deployment, having landed in the heat of the now bustling port of Kantara. He found Egypt a refreshing change to the drabness of Western Europe.

In December the RFA supported the EEF and Anzacs in the assault on Bir Lahfan on the Sinai Peninsula. Woolf discovered that the movement of artillery pieces through the sand of the Egyptian desert was as challenging as through the mud of the Somme or Ypres. The RFC flying overhead provided intelligence on the camouflaged Turkish redoubts of Magdhaba where the garrison was overrun before Christmas. Despite good railways, water and other essentials were in short supply, and illness was taking its toll.

At Christmas in 1916 it is quite likely that Barnato played in both a football match and a cricket match between British and Australian troops. The football was a draw, and despite Barnato's talent as a wicket keeper the Australians won the cricket.

In January 1917 preparations began for the assault on Rafa, on the border of Palestine and Egypt. Barnato and his RFA unit moved their guns into position for an artillery barrage, which commenced at 9 am on the 9th. The Turks and Germans appeared to be on the run, lifting Allied morale and motivating the troops to push hard against their enemy. The local Bedouins looked on unmoved as the battle raged. After taking Rafa, the advance to Beersheba was next, and the thought would have struck Barnato that he was about to battle for the Jewish homeland of Palestine. He received temporary promotion to captain and was tasked with supervising the daily routines of maintenance, cleaning, preparing the guns, and writing to the families of soldiers killed in battle.

In spring 1917 the next objective was Gaza, and the RFA unit was now reduced to two batteries. The battle for Gaza was fought twice, withdrawing the first time for fear of not being able to supply the force that had taken it.

In April Barnato became a full captain and his battery was withdrawn back to England. After sailing safely to Egypt, his convoy was attacked by a German battleship and submarine with the loss of one troop ship.

After a period of leave he returned to France and to Ypres. The success of the 'rolling barrage' in the Battle of Arras in April/May 1917 meant that his batteries employed the same tactic to support the advance at Passchendaele.

Woolf's battery was part of the combined barrage of over 3,000 guns that pounded the enemy for ten days before the Third Battle of Ypres. However, the rain of that summer – downpours not seen for thirty years – coupled with the fact that three years of artillery action had destroyed the agricultural drainage systems, made the movement of his guns nearly impossible. As the batteries moved to support the infantry, with the Germans holding the high ground at Passchendaele and the other ridges, Barnato lost some of his men to sniper fire. The Third Battle of Ypres ended with the capture of the Passchendaele Ridge in late November.

As the war moved into 1918, Barnato continued to serve through the influenza outbreak that commenced in February, and then the Kaiser's offensive between March and June 1918. Barnato's unit supported operations in Arras and Cambrai, driving the Germans back after their offensive had flagged.

Having come through the war relatively unscathed, just seventeen days before the Armistice his brother Jack succumbed to the Spanish flu.

It was early 1919 before he returned home, to live the life that had been delayed for four years. His life from then on would involve all kinds of competition and achievement.

Woolf immersed himself totally in any new sport he adopted, practising endlessly, taking lessons only from the very best instructors until he mastered it. Indeed he applied this attitude to all aspects of his life, including commerce, the racetrack, and love.

Woolf collected many prizes, including the 1925 Duke of York Trophy for motorboat racing, using his Bentley-powered *Ardenrun V*. He was a keen shot, he bred horses at his house, Ardenrun, and hunted with the Old Surrey and Burstow Foxhounds.

Ardenrun Place, near Lingfield in Surrey, was a 350-acre country estate constructed in the late 1900s. It was to achieve notoriety not only as the country house of Woolf Barnato, but also as the de facto home of the Bentley

Boys, the hard-driving, hard-partying playboys who epitomised the cocktail-fuelled decade-long party that was the roaring twenties. It was his former commanding officer who secured the house and grounds for him – he lived in a house on the Ardenrun estate.

Barnato set about the business of joining the landed gentry with gusto, expanding the estate to 1,000 acres and adding a golf course. Under Barnato's ownership Ardenrun became a 'playboy's' mansion. He built a full-size mock-Tudor pub in the rambling basement, complete with Elizabethan-style leaded windows with diamond panes, behind which were electric lights to create the impression of daylight. A large oak-beamed fireplace was festooned with pewter tankards. It was patronised by the rich and the famous of the time, including, for example, Fred Astaire.

As well as a boxer, Barnato was also a strong swimmer and played tennis to 'country house level'. He took golf lessons at Coombe Hill Golf Club with the club professional Archie Compston, a friend of the future King Edward VIII.

In 1917 Woolf claimed a share of the family business profits from 1897 to 1916 and broke off his business arrangements with the Joel family. After a long legal dispute in South Africa, Woolf settled for £900,000 plus £50,000 in costs.

Following settlement of the case, Woolf Barnato played first-class (professional) cricket, appearing as wicketkeeper with Surrey CCC from 1928 to 1930.

He began motor racing in 1921, when after importing an eight-litre Locomobile from the United States, he signed up to race at the Brooklands Easter meeting.

Having come third in a 100-mile race, he then swapped to a Calthorpe to compete at the following Whitsun meeting. For the 1922 season he bought a 1921 Talbot from its owner and driver Sir Malcolm Campbell, and for 1923 a car that Sir Alastair Miller customised for racing, a Wolseley Racing Moth. At the start of the 1924 season Barnato obtained an eight-litre Hispano-Suiza H6C chassis, which he commissioned Jarvis of Wimbledon to build a suitable racing body for. He then established an eight-litre class racing record for the car.

In late 1924 Barnato obtained a prototype Bentley 3.0 litre chassis, to which Jarvis fitted a boat-tail body at a cost of £400. He won several major Brooklands races with it, and then, partnered by fellow 'Bentley Boy' John Duff, he set a new 3.0 litre 24-hour record averaging 95.03 miles per hour at the Autodrome de Montlhéry.

When in 1925 Barnato purchased a 3.0 litre Bentley from the company, the company of Bentley Motors was in trouble. W.O. Bentley was too focused on the product he had created and not on the company finances. Head of sales A.F.C. Hillstead, aware of Barnato's considerable wealth, saw an opportunity; Barnato might be keen on acquiring his own marque and team. W.O. made the initial contact, on the pretext that Hillstead would bring the latest 6½ litre Bentley to Ardenrun Hall for a demonstration. Barnato was still asleep in bed as Hillstead drove the new model up the estate's extensive driveway across the golf course. Getting out of bed Woolf took the new car for a spin and then settled down to lunch with Hillstead.

Barnato was without doubt more of a sportsman than businessman, but he was aware of the value of money. He was also shrewd, well informed and well advised. He was renowned for being quite mean, loathing to offer anyone a cigarette: Bertie Kensington Moir, who raced at the 1925 Le Mans, said, 'He offered me a cigarette from his gold case that he kept in especially tailored pockets in his suits, and I am carrying the scars of the slamming of the flange of that case on my knuckles for life.'

His offer came in May 1926, Barnato initially invested £100,000, saving the company and its workforce. Then the original Bentley company was wound up, with all the creditors paid off and with existing shares devalued from £1 to just 1 shilling, or 5% of their original value. Barnato held 149,500 of the new shares, meaning that he controlled the company and became chairman. W.O. described this deal as 'a nasty knock for many of us', but at least his brand had survived.

Within months, Barnato faced his first challenge. The General Strike occurred in the month of his acquisition, between 4 and 12 May. Strike action affected rail services, and the big names in motorsport, including Malcolm Campbell and John Cobb, got involved in the national effort to drive buses and goods.

Within two days of the strike commencing, Barnato (with the police) formed 'The Brooklands Squad', a team of elite racing drivers using cars capable of 100 mph attached to Scotland Yard and entrusted to transport sensitive documents at high speed across the country. Also involved were Sir Henry Segrave and Frazer Nash, amongst others. These men completed many recorded and unrecorded driving feats in this role. The *Daily Mail* wrote: 'Capt Woolf Barnato took an urgent message from London to Birmingham, a distance of 106 miles, in two hours and eleven minutes,' which was only eleven minutes slower than the fastest express train of the day.

Barnato was estranged from his first wife, the daughter of a Wall Street financier, and thoroughly enjoyed life as a bachelor. It was said that no respectable girl should accept a lift home with Barnato after an evening out. One limousine of his, for nocturnal use, had a single seat compartment for the driver while the rest of the car was converted into a large L-shaped boudoir, equipped with curtains for privacy. One person described him as 'a laughing, mahogany tanned cavalier with wavy dark hair and brown eyes. He stood over six feet tall but looked shorter because of his stocky and muscular build.' Typical of the women he entertained in the back of this sumptuously appointed luxury vehicle was musical star June Tripp, whose hit songs included *Ladies Are Running Wild*. Barnato's life could be followed vicariously through the pages of society magazines such as *Tatler*.

Under Barnato's stewardship, what had become an underfunded, low volume, niche British carmaker was transformed. With friends like Fred Astaire and actor Jack Buchanan, and his cars driven by the Prince of Wales and Prince George, Bentleys became a must have for the international elite.

He poured money into Bentley's racing programme and, thanks also to his skill as a driver, the winged 'B' of Bentley came to dominate the winner's podium at the 24 Hours of Le Mans race so entirely that this unremarkable French town would forever become a little bit of England.

W.O. Bentley on Barnato: 'Once he took up a sport, he applied himself with religious concentration to the most elementary principles up to mastery. He won a wager that he could reduce his golf handicap from seven to scratch within a year, and he did. But what made him such an outstanding driver were his keen eye and judgment, his courage, discretion and self-discipline.' He also submitted with docility to team discipline. As chairman it would have been all too easy for him to have demanded the best car and the best pit crew, but he didn't. Again W.O.'s view: 'As a driver he regarded himself as an ordinary member of the team, accepting if need be to be second string without demur, suggesting by his manner and attitude that it was something of a privilege to have been included at all.'

The 1926 race season, even with Barnato's takeover, was not a glorious one for the Bentley marque, and without Barnato it is unlikely the marque would have survived. But the 1927 season saw the team 'turn professional'. A separate racing division was formed, drivers watched cine footage of pit procedures to improve performance, quick-filling fuel caps were developed, and timekeepers were given back-up stopwatches. Victory at Le Mans was the primary goal.

Barnato did not race at Le Mans in 1927 as he had a business matter to deal with that June in London. The race was won by a Bentley crew, Dr Dudley 'Benjy' Benjafield and fellow Great War veteran 'Sammy' Davis. In recognition of Benjafield's hard-fought victory in an accident-packed race, Barnato made a substantial donation to St George's hospital where Benjy worked as a bacteriologist.

The 1928 season saw the Bentley team include the Grosvenor Square 'Bentley Corner' residents, Tim Birkin, Glen Kidston, Bernard Rubin, and of course Woolf Barnato. Bentley won again with Barnato and Kidston in a 4½ litre with Birkin finishing fifth. A huge celebration dinner took place six weeks later, in the rather surprising venue of the Lyons Corner House in Coventry Street, and the assembled crew all signed a menu of the evening's fare. Bentley, Benjy, Kensington-Moir and Frank Clement also signed. That menu card sold at auction for £2,990 in 2006.

The win increased Barnato's celebrity standing further still. He was invited to endorse a brand of cigarettes and revelled in having his picture taken and signing autographs. He loved his racing, he loved to win, and he loved the limelight, but he was said to be gracious in defeat. It just didn't happen very often.

With Bentley winning Le Mans for two years consecutively, the British racing green Bentleys were hot favourites, and sure enough the 1929 Le Mans saw Bentley take the first four places. Barnato again took the victory, this time with co-driver and fellow socialite Sir Tim Birkin. Kidston took second place this time. Another of the icons of this book finished in sixth just behind the Bentleys, Robert Benoist. The rest of the season for Barnato and the boys was one long party, frequently hosted at Ardenrun Hall, the now HQ of this bunch of thrill and fun seekers.

On 24 October 1929 the stock market on Wall Street crashed. By noon the NYPD had deployed riot police to the financial district and by the end of the day eleven financiers had killed themselves, but for the likes of independently wealthy Barnato and other Grosvenor Square boys the crash didn't have much impact on their lifestyle.

As a driver, Barnato won the 24 Hours of Le Mans race three times: in 1928 with Bernard Rubin in a Bentley 4½ litre, in 1929 with Sir Henry 'Tim'

Birkin in a Bentley Speed Six, and finally in 1930 with Glen Kidston in another Bentley Speed Six. These were the only years he entered the race, leaving Barnato as the only Le Mans driver with a perfect wins-to-starts ratio. Bentley under his chairmanship had also won the race in 1927, so he could be credited with four consecutive wins.

Barnato later won the Brooklands Six Hour Race and Double Twelve Race in 1930. He was regarded by W.O. Bentley as 'The best driver we ever had and, I consider, the best British driver of his day. One who never made a mistake and always obeyed team orders.'

With the rise of the Cote D'Azur, or the French Riviera, becoming a holiday destination for the well-to-do in the early 1920s, a train service was established. Painted blue, *Le Train Bleu* carried the wealthy from the north of France to the south in absolute luxury. By the end of the 1920s 'the blue train races' was established, a challenge whereby gallant and competitive motorists would try to beat the train. In 1930 first a Rover and then an Alvis raced the train and won, the Alvis by three hours, the Rover by twenty minutes. Barnato was irritated by this and declared, 'This achievement does not deserve such merit.'

In March 1930 at the Carlton Hotel, Cannes, during the height of the Blue Train Races, Woolf Barnato raised the stakes. He claimed that he could not only beat the Blue Train from Cannes to Calais, but could reach London in his 6½ litre Bentley Speed Six before the train even reached Calais, and he was prepared to wager £100. There were no takers for the bet, but he decided that he was going to enter the challenge anyway.

He set off from the bar of the Carlton Hotel at just before 6 pm on 13 March. Accompanied by his friend Dale Bourne as unofficial co-driver, he decided not to follow the same route as the train. Research had shown him that the train made an hour stop in Marseilles, and then took three and half hours to cross Paris. Barnato and Bourne stopped for fuel at Aix-en-Provence, Lyon, Auxerre and Paris. They arrived at the docks in Boulogne at 10:30 am on the 14 March, in time for the 11:30 am sailing to Folkestone. Barnato reached Dale Bourne's club in St James's at 3:30 pm, having covered the 830 miles in 22½ hrs at an average speed of 43.43 miles per hour. Barnato drove an H.J. Mulliner-bodied formal saloon in the race. He had arrived four minutes before the train arrived in Calais.

The Wall Street Crash did effect the Bentley business, with the Great Depression reducing demand for the company's expensive products. In July

1931 two mortgage payments on the firm that were guaranteed by Barnato fell due, and accepting the inevitable he advised the lenders that he was 'unable to meet these debts'. On 10 July, on the application of the mortgagee the court appointed a receiver to Bentley Motors Limited. For a time it appeared that Napier was going to acquire the business, but in the end it passed into the hands of Rolls-Royce in November 1931 for the sum of £125,000 after a sealed bid auction.

Barnato received £42,000 in return for his shares in the business, having bought a sizeable stake in Rolls-Royce not long before Bentley Motors was liquidated. By 1934 he was again on the board of Bentley Motors Ltd.

In the Second World War Barnato continued various low-key business opportunities out of his office on Park Lane. But in March 1940 he attended an interview with Air Vice Marshall Keith Park at 11 Group RAF at their HQ at Uxbridge. The role he was offered was to coordinate the protection of the twenty-five airfields of 11 Group in the south of England, as they were vulnerable to attack, and also because they could be used as landing grounds by an invading force. He was offered the rank of wing commander for this appointment, equivalent to his former army rank of captain.

With Barnato as the lead, his team of five took responsibility for five airfields each. They were tasked with the construction of such things as blast pens to protect planes on the ground, and coordination with observation posts and the early warning radar system. There was also the construction of pillboxes to defend against landing by the enemy to be considered, and the commissioning of diggers ready to tear up runways if there was a chance of successful invasion. The defence of airfields was intensified after the retreat from Dunkirk.

Barnato continued to live at his Grosvenor Square flat during the Battle of Britain and Blitz, sheltering when necessary at an air raid refuge at the nearby Connaught Hotel. His cousin Dudley Barnato Joel, RNVR, who had been instrumental in his appointment in the RAF, was killed in May 1941 in the sinking of HMS *Ragistan*. His daughter, Diana Barnato Walker, joined the Air Transport Auxiliary in November 1941, and qualified as a pilot to begin delivering aircraft in May 1942.

Also in May 1942 Barnato was involved in the preparation of airfields for the imminent arrival of the USAAF, 8th Bomber Command. He spent his time between their intended headquarters at Bushy Park and RAF Bomber Command HQ at RAF Daws Hill.

The war drew him closer to his daughter Diana. They frequently spent time together at his new house in Englefield Green called 'Ridgemead'.

Woolf Barnato was married three times. His first wife was Dorothy Maitland Falk, to whom he was married between 1915 and 1933. They had two daughters, Virginia and Diana. His second wife was Jacqueline Claridge Quealy, whom he married in 1933. It lasted until 1947. The couple had two sons, Michael Jay and Peter Woolf. He married (thirdly) Joan Jenkinson in December 1947.

As mentioned, Barnato's daughter Diana Barnato Walker joined the ATA. She initially learned to fly at the Brooklands Flying Club in 1938 at the age of 20. She went on to ferry Spitfire and Hurricane fighters and Wellington bombers throughout the war. During her service she met her first fiancé, who was killed in combat. She then married, but her husband was tragically killed after the war but while still in RAF service.

When married to Dorothy Maitland, Barnato lived mostly at his house in Elsworthy Road, Hampstead. After their separation he lived at his flat at 50 Grosvenor Square in Mayfair, the so-called 'Bentley Corner'.

Ardenrun Place was destroyed by fire on 14 March 1933. It was after that in 1938 that he built the large castellated home named Ridgemead in Surrey. Designed by Robert Lutyens, son of architect Sir Edwin Lutyens, Ridgemead featured innovations such as central heating, a 'talkie' cinema and a driveway lit by secret lighting. It had 25 bedrooms, a heated swimming pool and was set in twenty-five acres of land overlooking the River Thames at Runnymede. After Barnato's death in 1948, his wife Joan sold the house for £25,000 and it became a nursing home, which it remains.

Barnato died at the London Clinic, Devonshire Place, on 27 July 1948 as a result of a thrombosis brought on after an operation for cancer. He was just short of his fifty-third birthday. His funeral cortège was led by his racing Bentley 'Old Number One', which was covered with flowers and wreaths. He is buried at St Jude's Church in Englefield Green. When his daughter Diana died, she also chose this spot for her and her husband, and as a result she was laid to rest with her father and husband.

The Blue Train episode gave Barnato acclaim and a position in society that no amount of money could have bought. His grandfather may have been an impecunious second-hand clothes dealer in the slums of London; his father may have been a brash nouveau-riche randlord of the South African diamond mining boom; but one Woolf 'Babe' Barnato, thanks to his acts of brazen derring-do, will forevermore remain in the pantheon of British 'have a go' heroes.

This was his obituary in *Motor Sport Magazine*, September 1948:

It was with real and heartfelt regret that we learned of the death of 'Babe' Barnato, following an operation at a London nursing home, at the age of 53. To all enthusiasts Woolf Barnato, son of 'Barney' Barnato, the diamond millionaire, is associated with the Bentley in the hey-day of 'the wearing of the green'. He made the fastest time at Le Mans in 1928 in a 4½-litre Bentley, partnered by Bernard Rubin. He won again in 1929, handling a 6½-litre in company with Sir Henry Birkin. And he did the hat-trick in 1930, winning a magnificent race again in a 6½-litre with Glen Kidston as co-driver. Barnato won the J.C.C. 'Double Twelve' in a 6½-litre Bentley, sharing the car with F.C. Clement.

Barnato commenced his racing career at Brooklands after the Kaiser war, racing Locomobile, Calthorpe, Mercedes, Austro-Daimler, Talbot, Ansaldo, Wolseley, Enfield-Allday, Bugatti and Bentley cars. He broke records in Hispano Suiza and Bentley cars. He joined the Board of Bentley Motors, Ltd., a position he held to the end. His chauffeur-driven Mk. VI Bentley saloon was a valuable ambassador for British products wherever 'Babe' travelled in recent times. He was president of the Bentley Drivers' Club and a founder-member of the B.R.D.C. Always fond of big fast cars, such makes as Hispano Suiza, Bentley and Rolls-Royce figured in his stable down the years. After giving up racing he acted in various official capacities and was directly responsible for the Barnato-Hassan race car at Bentley. Well known in London society and sporting circles, Barnato did his share of high speed on the water in the middle twenties. He served as a captain in the 1914-18 war and as a wing-commander during the Hitler trouble.

A pleasant personality, with an unassuming nature and a great relish for the sport in all its forms, Barnato retained a useful memory of cars and personalities.

You had to get up early and or drive hard right through the night if you wanted to beat Woolf Barnato. Either that or play for Lancashire's County Championship-winning cricket team of 1928.

Chapter 2

Sir Tim Birkin (1896-1933)

Royal Flying Corps in the First World War

Creator of the 'Bentley Blower'

Le Mans winner & Bentley Boy

Henry Ralph Stanley 'Tim' Birkin, born 26 July 1896, was a British Great War pilot and racing driver, becoming another of the 'Bentley Boys' in the 1920s.

He was born into a wealthy family in 1896, the son of Sir Thomas Stanley Birkin, 2nd Baronet, and the Honourable Margaret Diana Hopetoun Chetwynd. The family made their fortune in the lace trade and lived in Park House, Mapperley, Nottingham. In childhood Henry Birkin gained the nickname 'Tim' after the extremely popular children's comic book character 'Tiger Tim' created by Julius Stafford Baker. The nickname stuck for all his life.

Tim joined the Royal Flying Corps in the First World War, although his enlistment is with the 7th Battalion The Nottinghamshire & Derbyshire Regiment, the famous 'Sherwood Foresters'. This followed a three-year engineering course at Nottingham University College, in Shakespeare Street, Nottingham. His RFC records show that Birkin attended the London and Provincial Flying School at Hendon in August 1916, gaining his Royal Aero Club certificates. Having joined the corps by October 1916 he soon flew in a Sopwith two-seater, an RAE BE-2 and a Maurice Fairman Shorthorn. He was also signed off in elementary gunnery. On 16 January 1917 he was assigned to 81 Squadron and posted to Egypt. His records indicate repeated periods from August 1917 of being unfit for duty as a result of malaria. He appears to be not fit for air service between 1 August 1917 to 6 March 1918, even being hospitalised during February 1918.

It is easy to picture the RFC flying over the trenches of the Somme, or the muddy battlefields of Flanders, but the RFC squadrons were also deployed to the Middle East and even to the Balkans. In July 1916 the Middle East Brigade of the RFC was formed, concentrating RFC units to be based in Macedonia, Mesopotamia, Palestine and East Africa under one unified command. In the Middle East, units had to make do with older, often obsolete equipment, only later being given more modern aircraft. The Palestine Brigade of the RFC was formed in October 1917 to support the ground offensive against the Ottomans in Palestine. Despite their relatively small numbers the RFC gave valuable assistance to the army in the eventual defeat of Ottoman forces in Palestine, Jordan and Mesopotamia, modern day Iraq.

In July 1918, still in 'The Middle East', which might be Egypt, which features for a single record entry, or is possibly Palestine as recorded by other research, Tim was an assistant flying instructor and a pilot of the latest Sopwith, the 'Dolphin'. He remained fit for service (FFS) into January 1919, and then he is described as 'fit for ground service' for three months, when perhaps he suffered a relapse again. At the end of June he was invalided back to the UK and on 29 July 1919 he resigned his commission. Palestine is where he is recorded as having contracted malaria, and he would suffer its effects for the rest of his life.

He probably met Woolf 'Babe' Barnato in the Middle East. They had much in common, both very rich, both keen sportsmen, and both interested in cars and racing. Birkin was noted as a crack shot as well as a fast driver.

After his war service Tim married Audrey Latham, daughter of Sir Thomas Paul Latham, 1st Baronet, and Florence Clara Walley, on 12 July 1921. He and Audrey had two daughters. He was appointed full lieutenant on a reserve commission on 16 April 1926 to the Norfolk and Suffolk Yeomanry, a territorial regiment.

Tim and Audrey bought Tacolneston Hall in Norfolk where he enjoyed shooting and farmed. Birkin held his own with Barnato for having a hard-partying lifestyle on his estate, often duck shooting at night and playing improvised rugby in the house. Audrey, however, was not happy with his behaviour and his philandering. Birkin was caught with another woman at a hotel in Blakeney Point and in 1927 Tim and Audrey divorced.

It was in 1921 that he had turned to motor racing, competing in a few races at Brooklands. He raced a French marque called DFP (Doriot, Flandrin & Parent), and was known to W.O. Bentley and his brother Herbert as Herbert was a DFP agent. But business, marriage and family pressure forced him to retire from the tracks until 1927, when he returned in a 3.0 litre Bentley for a six-hour race as one of the 'Bentley Boys'.

Most of the time Tim presented a charming and aristocratic persona, but there was a dark side to him. He was shy, prone to bouts of depression, he stammered, and was conscious of his slender build and lack of height. He was described as 'ruthless, with his cars and everybody'.

Birkin was known for his stylish appearance as much as he was for his flair for driving at speed. Young men of the day looking for style trends observed that he was impeccably turned out in a checked tweed sports jacket and grey flannel trousers. He would take his good friend the Prince of Wales, another fashion icon of the day, to visit his factory workshops. He took equal care of his driving ensemble, wearing a dark blue sports shirt, white overall-style trousers and a distinctive spotted scarf. He wore his hair slicked back and sported a pencil moustache. When he raced he sported a white safety helmet based on an iron-age design that contained a St Christopher emblem inside it. Bizarrely he also sucked on oranges during races, discarding the husks in the footwell.

In 1927 he raced alongside his brother Archie. They had both bought Bentleys at the end of 1925. Tim bought another in February 1927, perhaps to celebrate his divorce. They entered the Essex Six Hour race at Brooklands, but Archie drove badly leaving Tim to drive alone, until a breakdown of a team Bentley led to Tim Birkin sharing his drive with Frank Clement. They finished third. Archie was tragically killed months later in practice for the 1927 Isle of Man TT.

In 1928 Tim became a works Bentley driver, joining the ranks of the high-profile Bentley Boys that included Babe Barnato, Glen Kidston and Bernard Rubin, all of whom were fellow Great War veterans. At Le Mans he drove a 4½ litre Bentley, leading the first twenty laps until a jammed wheel forced him to drop back, finishing fifth at the end of the race. He had blown a tyre that wrapped itself around the axle and brake drum buckling the wheel, delaying him three hours.

The 1929 Le Mans saw Birkin back as winner, racing the 'Speed Six' as co-driver to Woolf Barnato. The race could be seen as a procession of Bentleys with the team taking first, second, third and fourth places. Birkin's rash 'pressing on' driving style was complemented by Barnato's more measured approach to achieve victory.

The wealthy drivers with their carefree attitudes could cause friction with the mechanics. Frank Clement, although a driver, was not a man of means, and had a role in the mechanical maintenance of the cars. Of Birkin he said, 'He's a lone wolf, a car wrecker and not for anything would I ride with Birkin.'

Another pit crew mechanic observed of Birkin: 'When he filled up the tanks with cans they used to come flying back in the pits like cannon balls, and I often felt like shying them back at him.'

Birkin was also a problem where the pits were concerned due to his female entourage, prompting W.O. Bentley to instruct his pit manager to enforce 'No one in the pits except those authorised'.

Again all things changed for all the Bentley Boys after the Wall Street Crash. Birkin moved out of the Norfolk estate as his means were running short following his divorce, his racing, living the high life, and investing in car development.

In 1929 he had established his own motor works in Welwyn Garden City. He was keen, with the complete disapproval of W.O., to boost the performance of the 4½ litre by fitting a supercharger. Bentley's view was, 'To supercharge a Bentley is to pervert its design and corrupt its performance.' Birkin engaged with the Amherst Villiers' company, and with Barnato the de facto owner of the marque Birkin persuaded him to produce fifty 'blowers' to enable the Blower Bentley to enter Le Mans.

At the end of the 1920s wealthy spinster socialite Dorothy Paget had become interested in motor racing following a visit to Brooklands. She visited Birkin's motor works in October 1929 and soon became a sponsor for Birkin's project, providing finance and taking instruction from the incurably louche and soon to be knighted Sir Henry Ralph Stanley Birkin, colloquially still known as Tim.

Success in competition was not Birkin's only motivating factor with his blower project. He, like all his Bentley peers, was a patriot and wanted to showcase the best of what the British motor industry could produce due to what he described as the 'present lethargy in the UK motor industry'. He was frustrated by what he regarded as an indifferent attitude to Britain's standing in international motorsport. He found it appalling that Britain had never sported an official Grand Prix racing car and felt the country should field a pure racing machine.

Birkin could be considered quite forward thinking in his view that supporting a racing effort and fielding a team brought interest in the industry and sales: 'Race and win on Sunday, sell cars on Monday'. He also saw the entente that could develop between countries with the international racing scene, and the boost to other microeconomics if thousands flocked to races supporting businesses in those areas.

His relationship with Dorothy Paget endured and there is speculation that the two were romantically linked, despite her declared lifelong aversion to men, her unglamourous appearance and desire to live life as she wanted, but they did spend much time together. Her obituary in *The Sporting Life* reads, 'when she pulled out of Birkin's team in 1931 she was not entirely with a whole heart.'

Birkin's motivation for the creation of the supercharged Bentley was born out of the success of the supercharged Mercedes driven by Rudolf Caracciola at the end of the 1920s. In 1928 at the Nürburgring, Bentley had been outclassed by the Mercedes, to Birkin's frustration. W.O. Bentley remained resolute in not resorting to fitting a supercharger, but Birkin always spoke well of Caracciola: 'I can recall no time at which he has been guilty of recklessness or inaccuracy.'

In 1930 Bentley entered five cars, three factory-prepared cars and two of Birkin's blowers. W.O. had reluctantly entered into an agreement over the entry of the supercharged cars to defeat the Mercedes challenge. Interestingly, W.O. had entertained the thought of supercharging his 3.0 litre cars in 1924, and as Dr Dudley Benjafield recounted, W.O. himself assisted in the supercharging of the 4½ litre in the autumn/winter of 1929. In August 1929 W.O. had in fact ridden with Birkin as a mechanic in a blower at the Belfast TT where Birkin entered three cars and Kidston and Rubin crashed.

At a pre-race social gathering at Le Mans in 1930 the Bentley driver 'Sammy' Davis heard the Germans let slip they would try to limit the use of the supercharger. During the race, the flag dropping at noon on 21 June 1930, the Bentley team played on this admission by Mercedes. Birkin 'pressed on' passing the Mercedes, taking the lead but damaging a tyre in the process. But he had begun pressurising of the use of the rival's supercharger in so doing. He had to retire to repair the tyre allowing Caracciola to retake the lead, but during the night Woolf Barnato pushed the Mercedes hard, forcing Caracciola to use the power of the supercharger more and more. On the 83rd lap (each lap being ten miles) the Mercedes retired to the pits and did not emerge citing a dynamo failure. In line with W.O.'s ethos that the cars should go no faster than necessary to win, the Bentley team was able to ease its pace to take the win. Sadly for Birkin, the two Bentley blowers broke down late morning not far short of having completed the race.

After the 1930 Le Mans, Birkin took second place at the French Grand Prix at Pau driving a stripped-down supercharged Bentley, although at the end of the year he suffered a setback when Dorothy Paget withdrew her financial support. The blowers all got sold except one which Dorothy kept and allowed Birkin to race. He continued to compete in other marques and won Le Mans in 1931 in an Alfa Romeo. He received a telegram congratulating him from Benito Mussolini.

Birkin broke the Brooklands lap record in 1931: 'I was in Le Touquet with Babe Barnato where he bet me at dinner in the casino that I would not break the lap record at Brooklands. I flew to Brooklands where there was a crowd and I took the car round once to warm it up. After that I tried to never lift my foot from the accelerator. Over the bumpy surface I was once in the air for forty feet with the car. I did two laps at 134.6 mph and 135.3 mph and so set up a new lap record. I flew back to Le Touquet in the evening and had dinner back with Babe.'

After that Birkin's finances continued to decline. Birkin entered into partnership with businessman and racing driver Mike Couper, trading as Birkin & Couper Ltd. The company used the workshop in Welwyn Garden City for their general tuning and race preparation business, and for the manufacture of a miniature electric model racetrack, a precursor to modern slot car racing like 'Scalextric'. It was marketed under the name of Miniature Speedway. On 31 October 1932 Birkin & Couper Ltd closed and the company went into liquidation. In March 1933 the workshop at Broadwater Road, Welwyn Garden City, was put up for sale.

In 1933 he entered the Tripoli Grand Prix (having become Sir Henry Birkin that year). There were rumours the race was fixed, but Birkin managed to finish third. During the race while filling up the car with fuel he burnt both his arms on the exhaust. One witness account states that the Italians had removed pit equipment including a funnel that made filling the car with fuel more hazardous.

A few weeks later he was back in London. It was summer and he began suffering flu-like symptoms, becoming listless. Dr Benjafield, fellow driver, was consulted and initially thought he was going into a bout of depression, but noticed the dressings on his forearms and suggested medical care for potential blood poisoning. Birkin reluctantly agreed and was admitted to the Lady Caernarvon Clinic. Dudley Benjafield fought hard to save Birkin's life and he was recovering until suffering a relapse, but he died on the morning of 22 June. W.O. Bentley maintained in his autobiography that Birkin's death was not due to the burn but to the malaria he had contracted in the First World War which had sparked off septicaemia.

W.O. described Henry Birkin as 'a magnificent driver, absolutely without fear and with an iron determination, who, while there was anything left of his car, continued to drive it flat out and with only one end in view.'

The supercharged Bentley would eventually be immortalised as the personal favourite car of James Bond 007, who according to his creator Ian Fleming drove it with, 'an almost sensual pleasure'. The cost of developing the blower Bentley consumed most of Birkin's family fortune, and with his quest to race at every opportunity, it could be argued that it also cost him his life.

Chapter 3

'Sammy' Davis (1887-1981)

Chief Petty Officer RNAS in the First World War

Major REME in the Second World War

Le Mans winner & Bentley Boy

Sidney Charles Houghton Davis was born in South Kensington, London, on 9 January 1887, the son of Edwin and Georgina Davis. His father was a merchant and tea importer and his mother was a pioneer cyclist. He was educated at Westminster and University College London. While at prep school in Chislehurst, Kent, he met Malcolm Campbell, and on one occasion the duo were involved in a 'spectacular pile-up' with a borrowed penny-farthing bicycle.

Sidney was one of six children, but two female siblings died in their infancy. He, his brothers and remaining sister enjoyed a comfortable upbringing living in a house in Philbeach Gardens, Earl's Court. He enjoyed the tranquillity of the Little Cloisters adjacent to Westminster Abbey and sitting within the abbey in or near the chapel dedicated to Henry VII.

His comfortable upbringing had rewarded the family with reserved seating to watch the Diamond Jubilee Parade for Queen Victoria in 1897, in which they observed wave after wave of troops marching in review order. Among them was a contingent of German soldiers in gleaming silver-spiked Pickelhaube helmets.

In 1900 his father took him to observe a motor car trial event, and later that year his aunt let him steer her car as they drove along the Cromwell Road.

Sammy was a talented artist and so went on to the Slade School of Fine Art at the University of London, where by his own account he enjoyed an equitable existence with other students, commenting there was never any 'new boy' status.

His parents paid for him to take a trip to Paris in 1903, knowing he had an interest in cars, to watch the start of the Paris to Madrid race. He recounted that he saw some accidents but noted they were reported on an exaggerated basis in the UK press.

Through his school friends he had experienced driving one or two cars and had the long-term loan of a Rex motorcycle, all giving him the pleasurable sensation of mechanically-propelled speed.

By the time he was finishing his studies at the Slade the family had moved to Finchley in North London where the roads were somewhat quieter. He soon recognised that his interest in motor vehicles would cost money; he couldn't live off his parents for ever, art might not be a wealth-creating career, and he therefore needed a job.

In 1906 Davis became an apprentice with the Daimler Company following what he described as an 'intimidating interview' with managing director Sir Edward Manville.

Training as a draughtsman, he became involved with the design of the Daimler-Renard Road Train and Daimler's team of cars in the 1907 *Kaiserpreis* race. He was also involved hands-on in the construction and inspection of the cars, from brakes to fitting the drive-chains. Sammy spoke fondly of the staff on the shop floor, particularly of the foreman Mr Wormauld: 'I must have been a fine nuisance, but he was a character never to be forgotten, a little on the stout side but he knew the job from A to Z, he stood no nonsense and was formidable. But for no reason I can think of he took it upon himself to look after me vigorously.' He relates how a communist in the factory described him as 'that bleeding young aristocratic bastard,' but another shop floor worker said to the communist, 'Lay off him, he's learning and wants to work which is more than you do!'

It was at Daimler that he acquired the nickname 'Sammy'. Although of European origin, Sammy had an olive complexion, the purchasing department manager referring to him as 'this horrible dirty little boy' and 'little black sambo'. However, in later life they became friends. Her name was Molly Swain and Sammy credited her with teaching him more about life than anyone.

During this time he progressed through all aspects of vehicle design, build and development, and became an ardent motorcyclist entering hill climb events. He courted girls who also rode motorcycles, including one called

Muriel Hinde, 'who certainly could ride', but also recognising that he rode everywhere as if he was practising for a race.

While at Daimler he turned his artistic skills to good use by creating cartoons for the marketing department under the name 'Fleming'.

In 1910 he joined the staff of *The Automobile Engineer* magazine at Iliffe Publishing as a technical illustrator following a friend, Gordon Crosby, who had moved to *The Autocar* from Daimler. The pay was better, and Molly Swain's advice was 'Take it'.

He moved back to London, living in Bloomsbury with his office in Queen Street. Although his new job was illustrator, he was soon tasked with writing articles too, for which he rode with racing driver H.R. Pope in a 'Blue Train Race' in a car against a train leaving London Victoria for Turin. It was a hair-raising event in a grand prix car that had been rebodied as a four-seater to allow for a mechanic as well as Sammy. The car won in a time of 23 hours and 36 minutes. Sammy said that racing through France was better because 'the roads were quieter and they like that kind of thing'.

By 1912 Sammy was also a feature writer and sub-editor, and he was competing at Brooklands and spending most of his time with the racing community. Brooklands at this time was also becoming a hub for flying.

In July 1914 he travelled to France to attend the Grand Prix at Lyon and although having a riotous time, all was not well. The assassination had already taken place on 28 June in Sarajevo of Archduke Franz Ferdinand, so tensions were reaching a fever pitch between the Central Powers and the opposing Triple Entente. Although polite, he described an icy politeness between the French and German teams of Peugeot and Mercedes, with French hero Georges Boillot walking with 'an offensive swagger, like a modern D'Artagnan'.

Each lap at Lyon was 23.3 miles and included a bend called *le virage de la mort*. The race totalled 470 miles and Boillot led the race until the end when he had a mechanical failure and Mercedes swept the board coming first, second and third. Sammy noted that this was 'a victory that was not as pleasing as it should have been'.

He returned to the UK, to a meeting at Brooklands on 3 August, with the impending sense that there might soon be a world conflict. The very next day war was declared. Like many, he never gave a thought to the possibility of the UK being defeated in a conflict, and marched off to Whitehall to enlist as a private soldier, knowing he had been an accomplished marksman since his youth. But at 27 and with his technical background he was told by the army that he should take a commission. Eventually he was recruited into the Royal Naval Air Service and despatched a day later to Sheerness, dressed in blue and sleeping in a hammock. Next he was moved to the RNAS armoured car division and given the rank of chief petty officer, later attaining the commissioned rank of sub-lieutenant.

He was deployed to France as part of the Duke of Westminster's Squadron. He was satisfied by the comfort of armoured trucks with their quick firing guns and heavy machine guns. In May 1915 he was based at Neuve Chapelle where he witnessed chlorine gas attacks on the 9th. By then the armoured cars were able to support infantry actions in urban areas by clearing snipers and pockets of resistance.

The guns aboard the armoured vehicles were of small naval calibre and ejected their cartridge cases into the vehicles. These empty cartridge cases were supposed to be retained and returned to stores, but in combat they were often thrown from the vehicles. Sammy ended up travelling to Dunkirk to see a logistics captain to explain where the empty cartridge cases were, having previously given him the grid references of where to find them. They came to a satisfactory agreement that they had been 'lost overboard in heavy weather'.

He became interested in camouflage, designing a canvas screen painted to reveal a ruined building for use in the urban areas where the disruptive rural patterns used on the vehicles didn't work. Sammy described the actions as 'brisk' but also recognised many hours of boredom.

He had a cousin in the Border Regiment with whom he ventured to the front line and took part in the impersonal endeavour of sniping. He discovered how two snipers in opposing trenches might have a lull in proceedings, at least against each other, and would place a jam tin on top of their parapets to indicate a 'stand-down'.

In his biography he observed of warfare, 'The other bloke feels the same as you, is scared before an action starts like you, but is savagely exalted when the battle is in full swing.' He also felt that fighting was natural to man and in some ways was the finest expression of manhood. However, the enthusiasm and exuberance with which he had gone to war began to fade and he became despondent with inaccurate news reporting on military progress when in truth gains often only amounted to a few hundred yards.

Sammy was once required to attend a headquarters miles back and was disillusioned to see how well the high command was dining in a chateau far from the dangers and horrors at the front. He also saw friends and relatives die and began to doubt he would live to see the end of the war. But even through his fits of gloom he never failed to admire the courage of the fighting infantry, commenting, 'The Germans knew our troops were far too dangerous to interrupt their tea.'

In one period of leave he discovered (nearly all on a single day) that his father had died, his brother Hugh in the Royal Flying Corps had been shot down and killed in a 'berserk mood' attack on a German squadron, and his brother Cyril was killed in the Ypres Salient deadlock. He had also lost a cousin, two nephews and two uncles in the conflict.

After a period of convalescence having fallen sick he was transferred to aircraft engine maintenance with the Royal Naval Air Service at Humber Ltd in Coventry where he crossed paths with W.O. Bentley. They had met at Brooklands before the war and Bentley was working at Humber on a new rotary engine.

In 1918 he witnessed the birth of the RAF from the amalgamation of the RFC and RNAS. He noted how both units hated it, fiercely proud of their own branches, and initially many insisted on wearing their old uniforms.

Sammy underwent surgery that year to remove gallstones and his appendix. He was then sent to recuperate in Swanage to regain his strength and fitness. By now he was a captain.

On his return to normal life Sammy noted how there was a distinct divide between those who had been to war and those who hadn't, each being unable to understand the other. When he returned to Iliffe Publishing with a view to resuming his previous position he was quizzed about what his part in the war had been, so he exclaimed his involvement of aircraft engines. The reply was, 'Well, that's some use to us anyhow.' Sammy was furious, taking some hours to cool down.

Sammy had married Rosamund Pollard on 16 June 1917 at St George's, Hanover Square. He was 31 and she was 20.

He settled into work at Iliffe with a journal called *Light Car* as development of small engine cars was the trend for mass affordability. This also led to an increase in vehicle trial and racing competition at a lower level, but for Sammy this wasn't the racing he wished to compete in.

In September 1921 he was invited to drive at Brooklands to try to break a few records, including the famous 'Double-Twelve', two periods of twelve hours driving a six-cylinder two-litre AC. It was exactly the experience he was looking for, and although they didn't break the Double-Twelve they did set some smaller records for speeds of over 70 mph around the banked, oval circuit.

Sammy, writing under the name 'Casque', became the sports editor with *The Autocar*. He chose the name Casque as he claimed that he and Sir Henry Segrave were the first to wear crash helmets when racing. It was from this position that he assisted W.O. Bentley in establishing the Bentley Car Company.

With his growing profile in motorsport, in 1922 Sammy was part of Aston Martin's effort to break no less than 10 world records and 22 class records at Brooklands.

At Brooklands he met wealthy Count Louis Zborowski who invited Sammy to be his riding mechanic at the 1924 French Grand Prix at Lyon. Sammy's view of Zborowski's driving was 'a mite wild, but definitely exciting and good'. Among the other drivers was the legendary Sir Henry Segrave (fellow motorsport military hero) and one of the other motorsport military heroes profiled in this book, Robert Benoist. Sammy's account of their mechanical troubles through half the race until they were forced to retire reads like an MOT test for a barn find! They completed 16 laps while the finishers completed 35. It was won by Giuseppe Campari. Robert Benoist came third and Segrave fifth.

Sammy's racing career accelerated in 1925, starting with a test at Brooklands of a Sunbeam V12 18 litre producing 350 bhp which he described as 'making one feel like one was walking with the gods'. From this he was offered to partner the French driver Jean Chassagne at that year's 24 Hours of Le Mans. They came second to the French pairing of Andre Rossignol and Gerard de Courcelles in a Lorraine-Dietrich.

Sammy now graduated to becoming one of the legendary 'Bentley Boys'. He had his first official Bentley drive in 1926 at Le Mans with Dr Dudley 'Benjy' Benjafield in a 3.0 litre and came close to glory. However, pressing on with two laps to go, attempting a do-or-die overtaking at the end of the Mulsanne Straight, Sammy was too fast into the bend and crashed into the sandbank at Mulsanne Corner. It was impossible for him to dig it out on his own and Lorraine-Dietrich won again.

The next year was very different for Sammy and Dr 'Benjy'. They won the 1927 24 Hours of Le Mans outright, covering 1,472 miles at an average speed of 61.3 mph. *Motor Sport* magazine reported, 'The victory, in spite of the accident that crippled the 3.0 litre Bentley driven by J.D. Benjafield and S.C.H. Davis, will always remain an epic, and even if the competition was not as keen as in the past, it is a great thing to have won a race with a car which was damaged in the early part of the event.' During the race Sammy had broadsided a huge pile-up on the track, becoming the fourth vehicle in a collision at 'Maison Blanche'. Thankfully no one was killed from any of the three cars already involved, two of which were the other Bentleys, and Sammy limped the car to the pits for makeshift repairs that got them through the race and to victory. They celebrated in style with a huge banquet at the Savoy, their race-winning car being pushed into the dining salon! Bentley went on to win the next three Le Mans, with Woolf Barnato always at the helm.

Later in 1927 Sammy raced with Bugatti at the British Grand Prix at Brooklands against Robert Benoist in a Delage.

In 1928 he finished ninth at Le Mans in a revolutionary 1½ litre front wheel drive Alvis, and second in his class with co-driver Bill Urquhart-Dykes. The RAC announced a revival of the TT which had previously run between 1905 to 1922 on the Isle of Man but would now be held in Northern Ireland. Sammy drove a Riley along with other team drivers Chris Gallop and Chris Staniland, but due to crashes in the dry and then in the wet none of them finished.

In 1929 Sammy finished second overall and class winner in the Brooklands Double Twelve in a 4.0 litre Bentley partnered with Sir Ronald Gunter, with others of the 'Bentley Boys' also in the team, Barnato, Birkin and 'Benjy'.

He finished second again in 1930 in a 6.0 litre Bentley.

At Le Mans in 1930 he met with misfortune when his goggles were shattered by a stone, forcing his retirement, and there were concerns he might be blinded. It was this event that saw five Bentleys enter, three standard factory 6.0 litres and two 4½ litre supercharged cars from Sir Tim Birkin's stable. Bentley took first and second.

In the summer of 1930 Sammy was asked to partner Gwenda Hawkes in a race at the oval track at Montlhéry near Paris, a track where she was considered 'the reigning queen'. They drove a three wheeled Morgan. Gwenda, like Muriel Thompson, drove an ambulance during the First World War but on the Eastern Front, and was a motorcycle racer as well as a car racer.

In October 1930 Sammy partnered the Earl of March in an Austin Seven, winning the BRDC 500-mile race at Brooklands.

Sammy's so far almost unscathed career came to a brief halt in 1931 at an Easter race meeting at Brooklands. He had an accident in the rain driving in a low-chassis Invicta S-type, skidding into a telegraph pole support cable, having managed to miss the spectators, some railings and the actual pole. He broke a leg above and below the knee, as well as his goggles shattering with his nose bleeding. For a season, 1932, he turned to team management with Aston Martin, beginning with Le Mans.

In 1933 Sammy was back in the driving seat and finished seventh overall at Le Mans in an Aston Martin. He was increasingly turning his attention to team management, as well as continuing his 'day job' in journalism.

At the 1935 Tourist Trophy in Ards in Northern Ireland, Sammy was one of four drivers competing in a Singer Nine. During the race he noticed two of his teammates had crashed out, and being in his eyes very competent drivers he was concerned that perhaps they had both gone out with a mechanical failure. He was right. Going into part of the circuit called Bradshaw's Brae, and approaching one of the corners where fellow driver Alf Langley had crashed, as he attempted to steer for the bend he got no response from the car. He braced himself for a crash, and in so doing was prepared to leap from the car just before impact with the banking. In the very last second he slid over the back of the car, the vehicle just missing the spectators. It was discovered the crash was due to a broken steering ball joint. Sammy's car clipped the already stricken Singer of Langley, and despite the severity of the crash, Sammy was largely unhurt.

In April 1937 Sammy drove a BMW 328 around Brooklands, covering more than 102 miles in an hour at an average speed of 102.2 mph, the first time for a car in that class.

Sammy had a run in a racing boat in 1938, but his adventures in racing cars were over.

Although motor racing history has concentrated on Sammy's track racing career, from 1930 and certainly up to 1937 he competed regularly in rally events and was a regular finisher. He took part in the UK RAC rallies and Monte Carlo rallies on several occasions.

While in hospital after his 1931 Brooklands crash, Sammy wrote *Motor Racing*, one of many literary works he would produce.

As well as his serious journalistic books about racing and racers, Sammy also published more light-hearted books under his pseudonym 'Casque'. These were primarily a vehicle for Sammy's highly accomplished humorous cartoons of racing cars, drivers and their foibles, and the world of motor racing between the wars. It was his insider's view of racing, the fallibility of racing drivers, the incompetence of officials, and the unreliability of racing machines. His two sketchbooks include Brooklands, Le Mans, Alpine trials, the Monte Carlo Rally and the TT races. His *Expensive Noises* of 1950 features many exploding engines. Sammy would continue to attend racing events, write, and paint into his 80s.

He was the first vice-president of the Aston Martin Owners Club in 1935, designing the Aston Martin 'wings' badge. After the war, he did much to promote the revival of motorsport in Britain, both as vice-president of the Vintage Sports-Car Club and as president of the new 500 Club (later the British Racing and Sports Car Club). He was a committee member of the BRDC. He also served on the Competitions Committee of the Royal Automobile Club, the governing body of motor sport in the United Kingdom.

When war broke out in 1939 Sammy was aware he was too old to enlist, and the navy and the air force were also aware of his age from his previous service, so he became an air raid warden and enlisted as a reservist to a corps that would later become Royal Electrical and Mechanical Engineers (REME). His unit was the 53rd Infantry Troops Workshop, and he was initially based in Tidworth in Wiltshire. Later he transferred to REME workshops in Ashford, Kent, and became Major Davis. There he watched Home Guard recruits throwing beer bottles at a low flying Messerschmitt; and he and a colleague once lost control of a Covenanter tank, crashing it into a private tennis court. The owner was furious and they thought it better to remain inside the tank.

Sammy was given orders to prepare for deployment to France and began moulding his unit accordingly. He taught them marksmanship and improved their shooting skills considerably. On the point of deploying with 12 Corps, a young RAMC female doctor declared him unfit because he was too old; he was nearing 57. He roared off on his motorcycle to corps HQ to see the principal medical officer, who was most amused. He declared him fit, 'This officer is absolutely convinced he is completely fit, or quite mad. I have examined him with care and he is quite fit.'

Preparations continued, including practice beach landings in Dorset and erecting shelters for sleeping undercover. On one occasion his unit succeeded in shooting down what turned out to be an early V1 flying bomb; he opened up with tracer rounds while others around him used assorted weapons.

In France in 1944 Sammy's unit advanced to Arnhem, dealing with booby traps and mines. They experienced pockets of German resistance seemingly from 'both sides of the road' and their sniping skills were put to good use. Sammy was mentioned in despatches.

Following the success of American forces sweeping through the Falaise Gap, he took a trip in his Jeep christened 'Fifi' to Le Mans with two of his NCOs and was the first British officer to enter Le Mans following its liberation. In 1945 he crossed the Rhine with the Allied forces, observing white flags flying from almost every window. He said that some German soldiers fought 'darned hard and behaved well', while others were 'over-uniformed, unpleasant and thug-like'.

In Hamburg, on demobilisation he couldn't recall the age he had given on enlistment. He got it wrong and was immediately returned to London where, having obtained a birth certificate from Somerset House, he found his mother had also got his date of birth wrong!

Sammy observed that he had lost fewer friends in the Second World War than the First: 'Most of a generation had not disappeared in a way we all remembered too well from The Kaiser Trouble.' But he noted that some of the Brooklands set were lost serving with the RAF and that fellow driver Robert Benoist was 'murdered by the Nazis at Buchenwald Camp as a member of the resistance.'

He returned to *Autocar* as sports editor, continuing to write as 'Casque'. The world of motorsport slowly returned in the last years of the 1940s, Sammy stewarding for the *Rallye Gastronomique*, a pleasant run from vineyard to vineyard. In 1950 he retired from *Autocar* and became a freelance writer.

Sammy also took to driver training and was critical of parents who bought their privileged children a performance car as soon as they had passed their test. Once he witnessed someone pass a test in a Mini and then drive a sports car and have a fatal accident. He was criticised by a pupil for never having taken the test himself – Sammy's driving predated official tests. He promptly contacted the chief examiner and took and passed his test.

Sammy found work on television and radio. He was a technical advisor to a production filmed on the Pendine Sands, and was flown around the world by various motoring organisations as a highly respected motoring correspondent.

His first marriage to Rosamund, that had produced his son Colin in 1933, broke down and he married again, Susie, much younger than him, a former art student who shared his passion for art. They made their home in Guildford. Susie also shared Sammy's passion for cars and racing and in 1966 they competed in the London to Brighton rally in his three-wheeled Léon Bollée called *Beezelbub*. Sammy had been competing in that event since 1928.

Sammy in his biography, produced from his autobiographical notes by Peter Heilbron and Malcolm Jeal, had a fear of getting old and losing his mental and physical abilities. But his last photographic portrait was taken in 1975 at the age of 88 and in the picture his eyes and smile have a sparkle indicating an active and lucid mind.

Sammy died in a fire at his own home in January 1981 aged 94. He hoped there was a Valhalla to go to in the next life. His first wife Rosamund died later that year aged 78, and Susie died in July 1983, following him hopefully to his Valhalla.

Sammy wrote unpublished autobiographies in 1932, 1949 and the late 1960s. He was a founding member of the Aston Martin Owners Club, the British Racing Drivers' Club and the Veteran Car Club of Great Britain. Along with General Patton, Jacky Ickx and Derek Bell, he was made an honorary citizen of Le Mans, and like Robert Benoist had a street there named after him.

Sammy and Rosamund's son Colin became a noted racing car driver in his own right, beating Jim Clark and Denny Hulme in the 'Trofeo Mondiale' in 1959. He got two Formula One entries, won the Targa Flora in 1964, and competed at Le Mans with Jo Siffert.

In closing, the following was said about Major Davis by Artificer Sergeant Major Bramwell Taylor: 'We respected him for his intimate approach to his warrant officers and men alike, and loved him for his eccentricities and dogged spirit. Having broken most of the bones in his body, it did not prevent him from limping along on route marches. His life in the field was spartan, a biker's tent being his only abode, although I might add beautifully arrayed with his personal flags. Many a man became an expert marksman under his tuition.' Teaching driving is teaching a life skill but teaching how to increase your chances of survival in war is a calling.

Chapter 4

Captain John Duff (1895-1958)

Royal Berkshire Infantry in the First World War

Stunt man, record breaker and Le Mans-winning Bentley Boy

John Francis Duff was born on 17 January 1895 in Kiukiang, China, to Canadian parents John Lindsey Duff and Margaret Ostler who moved there in 1891 as Christian missionaries.

He was one of only two Canadians to win at Brooklands, the first Canadian to race in the 24 Hours of Le Mans, and the only Canadian to win overall at Le Mans.

He was 'very tall and lanky with a long face' and had the look of a classical adventurer, often standing defiantly with his hands on his hips and wearing a thick roll neck sweater and plus fours. In his life, among other things, he was an infantry officer, a fencing coach, a Hollywood stunt man, and one of the original 'Bentley Boys'. Bentley described him as 'a man with tremendous guts and determination', the pit crews' view was 'he had tons of guts'. His tenacity saw him promoted to captain swiftly in the Great War; he always led from the front.

At the age of 5 he went to live with his grandparents in Hamilton, Ontario, where he started school. At 16 he returned to Kiukiang an energetic, daring and rather wild adolescent. By all accounts he kept quite wild company. He had an association with a group of Russians in the summer of 1913 when the final stages of the civil war that had begun in China in 1908 were still raging. He and his Russian friends went out on some night patrols, returning one morning with a bullet hole through his hat and another through his sleeve. A *New York Times* article describes the following incident:

July 26th

A volunteer force of American and British are guarding the hilltop city of Kiukiang where around 2,000 UK and US nationals, mainly women and children, are sheltering from the Chinese summer heat. A small detachment of US blue jackets is maintaining communications from the hills. The foreigners in the city are able to observe the conflict outside. The Rt Reverend Logan H. Roots, the Bishop of Hankow, says the city is the safest place.

The refusal of Rear Admiral Reginald F. Nicholson, commander in chief of the American-Asian fleet, to send marines in is generally criticised in non-military circles, although the German and British admirals are reported to agree with him.

The American guard was agreed upon by all legations. The only danger seemingly arises from outlaws and dispersed soldiers attempting to loot. The American admiral has offered to escort the foreigners to the river.

These Russians were sons of the owners of the brick-tea factories in Hankow & Kiukiang. They bought racehorses in Hankow and roamed in the Liu mountains hunting wild boar.

As the Great War began in 1914, Russia on the side of the 'Allies' with France and Britain, Duff and his Russian friends joined a Cossack regiment, serving in the mountains. But after setbacks and facing the prospect of revolution in Russia, the Russian fathers sent their boys to Vladivostok and Duff went to England, where he joined the British Army.

By 1916 Duff was a first lieutenant in the Royal Berkshire Regiment (Princess Charlotte of Wales) 2/4th Battalion deployed on the front lines near the village of Hébuterne, on the northern end of the Somme battlefront. It was the scene of heavy, protracted trench warfare and saw diversionary attacks against the German forces on 1 July 1916 at the neighbouring village of Gommecourt.

On 22 May Duff led a wire-cutting mission into the no man's land. His group was spotted by the Germans and fired upon which killed many and wounded the rest of them. Duff received extensive wounds and was either rescued and returned to his front line or while wounded made his own way back to safety. His National Archives medical records show him evacuated from his unit to medical care in France on 23 May, and on 13 June he was repatriated to England aboard the *Cambria*.

He was admitted to British Red Cross Society, Brighton, on 4 September with

fever and two wounds discharging pus, one above the clavicle and the other over the upper dorsal spine. Under anaesthetic an opening made for drainage

in the right axilla diaphragm. Necrosis of the scapula at upper border and
further operations required. Right arm weak.
Limb loss or permanent eye injury: no
Severe wound: no
Effects still severe: yes
Permanence: uncertain.

On 20 October he was moved to the Queen Alexandra Hospital, Millbank, and was then hospitalised at Sussex Lodge Hospital, Regent's Park. His injury was recorded as a shell wound, but there is also reference to it as a gunshot wound.

Report dated 30ᵗʰ November 1916; Shell fragment into the 4ᵗʰ dorsal
vertebrae that exited front under the outer end of the clavicle traversing
the upper lobe of the lung. Fracturing both shoulder blade and collar bone.
'Haemophatophis' for a week after injury, bones now knitted. Front wound
healed but the second serious deep persisting in the back. Limited shoulder
movement.
Limb loss or permanent eye injury: no
Severe wound: yes
Effects still severe: yes
Permanent effects: no
Recuperation period: 3¼ months.

He never returned to front line duties.

On 12 March 1917 he was still unfit for general service and granted leave until 11 April. He was paid an injury gratuity of £125 on 10 April having been paid £104 as a first injury gratuity in September 1916. Finally in August 1918 he was classified as 'A' category for service but recommended to service in the cavalry or other mounted service. He was granted leave into September to report to Cambois in the north of England.

While recovering from his injuries Duff met a nurse who would become his wife, Clarissa 'Poppy' Lindsey. They married on 4 March 1917 at the Parish Chapel, St Pancras. Poppy had been Duff's nurse at the Endsleigh Palace Hospital for Officers. By 1920 their address was Portman Mansions, Paddington.

In 1919, John Duff learned how to drive a car and became a car dealer, and in 1920 started racing. Duff began his racing career at Brooklands, the 2.6-mile concrete track with steep concave banking. He drove a Fiat S61, a 10-litre chain-driven car built in 1908. By August he was lapping in the same time range as Sir Henry Segrave.

He won the May 1921 '75 Long Handicap' race there, averaging over 104 mph around the bumpy track, and then proved it was no fluke by winning the '100 Long Handicap' that summer, this time at 104.85 mph. His success attracted a penalty from the handicappers, and while always very quick, he was denied further successes in the S61.

Duff was an early supporter of W.O. Bentley's new motor company. His own venture, Duff & Aldington, became a Bentley dealer in 1922. He had met his partner William Aldington at Brooklands but they established a showroom at 10 Upper St Martin's Lane, London. Seeking to publicise the new marque he took a stock 3.0-litre model on a record-breaking drive at Brooklands. Twenty-four-hour running was not permitted at the Weybridge track, to allow the locals a decent night's sleep, but Duff later raised the double-12-hour record to 86.52 mph, covering 2,082 miles during the split stint. The event was depicted on the cover of the first edition of the *Brooklands Gazette* in July 1924. Overall he set thirty-eight international class records, a massive deal for the time, and for Bentley.

The accomplishment of the double-twelve came at a price. Although normally meticulous in preparation, he had made his own steel bucket seat without padding and with the peak of the upright of the seat sitting just below his shoulder blades, meaning it rubbed his skin raw over the twenty-four hours. The non-padded seat also meant his limbs went numb, which at one point while taking a break left him unable to adjust his clothes to satisfy a call of nature!

Duff believed not only in mechanical preparation for racing but also in physical preparation. He swam in the lake on Hampstead Heath, ran at least twenty miles a week, and for breakfast ate honey, followed by a raw egg cracked into his mouth, and lettuce leaves.

At the Brooklands autumn meeting of 1922, Duff appeared at the wheel of J.L. Dunne's old 21-litre Blitzen Benz. He lost the 100 Mile Handicap to rival Parry Thomas, despite lapping at 114.49 mph. Unable to stop the old car at the end of the last lap, he shot over the top of the banking and crashed through trees and a telegraph pole outside the circuit.

In 1923 Duff heard of the new 24-Hour race to be held at Le Mans. He was the first entrant to apply. W.O. Bentley thought it was madness and that no car could finish such a race, but in the face of Duff's determination he agreed to have a car prepared for him at the factory and let his test driver Frank Clement partner him. The Duff/Clement Bentley set the fastest lap at 9 minutes and 39 seconds for the 10.726-mile lap. Rough track conditions took their toll as a flying stone holed the fuel tank, forcing Duff to run back to the pits. As only the drivers could work on the cars, Clement had to bicycle back with a can of petrol to power the car back to the pits. Despite the drama, Duff and Clement finished a strong fourth, driving through heavy rain and hail on a dirt road. After that, W.O. Bentley, who attended the race at the last minute, became hooked on the Le Mans concept, the race that would make his cars world famous.

Duff then took his Bentley to the Spanish Touring Car GP at Lasarte in St Sebastien. Leading with two laps to go, he was hit in the face by a stone thrown up by a lapped car. Duff crashed into a wall, injuring his jaw and breaking some teeth. Despite that, he won first place in the 3.0-litre class, as he had easily outlasted and outdistanced his competition.

In 1924 Bentley was fully committed to Le Mans as a marque in their own right. However, Duff was still a private entrant, using one of the dealership's cars, a 3.0-litre that was works prepared, using ideas Duff had come up with after the 1923 race.

The race was moved to June from May in 1924 in the hope of better weather than the previous year, and there were rule changes by the organisers. Open cars had to stop at the pits on the end of the fifth lap to raise their hoods, after which they had to complete at least twenty laps with the hood deployed. Then the car had to return to the pits to be checked by officials. In preparation for this Duff practiced raising and fixing the hood and got his time down to forty seconds without even exiting the car. Regulations also decreed that only the driver could work on their car, including filling with petrol, oil and water, all delivered not by pipe but by heaving it from cans. In addition to working on his physical fitness to prepare for these tasks, Duff lagged the petrol tank to protect it from flying stones. He also fitted a mesh to protect the headlights and the radiator. It was from this that Bentley's criss-crossed radiator grill pattern was developed and retained as part of the marque. Partnered again by Frank Clement in a race run in intense summer heat, Duff won, giving Bentley its first victory at Le Mans.

Le Mans in 1925 did not have such a happy ending. Initially Duff ran out of fuel and against the rules dashed to his pits to refuel the car. When Bentley pointed out that it was against the rules, Duff replied in vigorous tone, 'It's my car and I'll do with it what I damn well like!' His race continued, but a carburettor fire ended his chances despite his attempts to smother it with a cushion. It was to be Duff's last Le Mans.

Later in the year Duff went to the banked French racetrack at Montlhéry for a race meeting over 9-10 September. He wanted to try for the absolute 24-hour record. Duff had a special single-seater body on his Bentley, and works driver 'Benjy' Benjafield was his co-driver. In driving rain, they did the first 12 hours at 97.7 mph, but they missed the 12-hour record. At 18½ hours the camshaft drive failed, ending the attempt. But he was, as a result of their endeavours, able to claim two world records: 1,000 kilometres in 6 hrs 23 mins 55 secs, and 1,000 miles in 10 hrs 15 mins 59 secs.

On 21 September Duff returned to Montlhéry with Captain Woolf Barnato – who, as already told, became the majority shareholder in Bentley and de-facto owner – as his co-driver. On a damp track in heavy mist they covered 2,280 miles in 24 hours, averaging 95.02 mph. They beat the previous record held by a 9-litre Renault by over 7 mph. Along the way the 3.0 litre Bentley took twenty-one world records, including those for six and twelve hours, and 500, 1,000, and 2,000 miles.

Looking for new challenges, Duff went to America on 8 March 1926, arriving in Buffalo, NY, on 16 June.

Duff signed to drive a Miller race car (built by Harold Arminius Miller, lauded as the greatest US race car builder of the day) sponsored by the Elcar Automobile Company, at the iconic endurance race, the Indianapolis 500. This followed the death of Herbert Jones, who was killed attempting to qualify in the Elcar Special. In a race shortened to 400 miles due to rain, Duff finished 9th.

The next AAA (American Automobile Association) championship event was on the 1.25-mile lap wooden board track at Altoona, Pennsylvania, on 12 June. Duff finished 3rd in the 250-mile race, two laps behind the winner.

The next race was on the Rockingham board track in Salem, New Hampshire, and was to be his last. A puncture pitched Duff's car sideways, throwing him from the car. His car crashed through the top rail of the banking and dropped clear off the track, Duff suffering a broken collar bone, as well as other painful bone and muscle injuries and a concussion that affected his vision. Knowing that his competitiveness would be compromised and having once promised his wife that he would quit if he suffered serious injury, he retired from racing.

Duff held over fifty world records for speed and endurance, sanctioned by the AIACR, Association Internationale des Automobile Clubs Reconnus, the forerunner of today's FIA. They included both class and absolute records. His achievements helped make the name of the Bentley car company in the 1920s. Duff scored a top-ten finish in his first Indianapolis 500 and a top three in his first board track race, classic North American races, those achievements making him one of the preeminent Canadian racers of all time. He was inducted in the Canadian Motorsport Hall of Fame.

John Duff enjoyed life in America, and settled with his wife and family in Santa Monica, California. There he opened, of all things, a fencing academy in Los Angeles, at which he trained numerous Hollywood movie stars. He had been selected for the British Olympic fencing team in 1924, the same year as his Le Mans success. He also began working as a stunt-double, doing Gary Cooper's sword fights in *Beau Geste*. He also taught fencing at UCLA and helped coach the 1932 US Olympic team.

The depression years of 1932-34 saw him leave Hollywood and resettle in China, where the family's interests in Kiukiang were doing well, before returning to England for 1935.

In England he continued fencing and car dealing. He also did well in steeplechasing and show-jumping, and remained successful and quite prominent in public life. But eventually his luck ran out. The 62-year-old John Duff was riding in Epping Forest on 8 January 1958 when he was thrown from his horse. He broke his neck and died.

The phrase 'the candle that burns twice as bright burns half as long' could be applied to Duff. His light was bright, and his personal achievements from dutiful sacrifice in war and setting world records were fearless and inspiring.

Chapter 5

Lieutenant Commander Glen Kidston (1899-1931)

Royal Navy in the First World War, submariner

Le Mans winner & Bentley Boy

George Pearson Glen Kidston was born on 23 January 1899 to Archibald Glen Kidston, a grandson of the founder of A.G. Kidston & Co, Glasgow metal and machinery merchants with interests in the Clyde Shipping Company, which grew into a banking concern that amalgamated into the Clydesdale Bank.

As a boy Glen was keen on the outdoor life. He attended a boarding school from where his letters home asked how many stags and grouse his father had shot and asked his mother to send him some white heather from the Scottish moors.

Kidston began his naval service in May 1912, a month after the *Titanic* had sunk, at the age of 13. He attended the Royal Naval College, Osbourne, on the Isle of Wight and then went on to the Naval College at Dartmouth. A report at age 15 says he 'promises to become a VG [very good] executive officer. Has brains, initiative, and shows great tact and command in leading men. VG knowledge of his duties.'

As a young midshipman he was torpedoed twice, in the sinkings of both HMS *Aboukir* and *Hogue* in the Battle of Heligoland Blight. These sinkings took place on the same morning, 22 September 1914. In an area of the North Sea known as the 'Broad Fourteens', U-boat *U-9* intercepted the three warships of the Seventh Cruiser Squadron. *U-9* fired off all six torpedoes, reloaded while submerged, and in less than an hour sank *Aboukir*, *Hogue* and *Cressy*. 62 officers and 1,397 men were killed, 837 survived. Kidston was aboard both and survived both.

He was captured and released, and then served on the dreadnought HMS *Orion* at the Battle of Jutland.

The Battle of Jutland was a naval engagement between the Grand Fleet of Britain's Royal Navy and Germany's Imperial Navy High Seas Fleet. The battle unfolded from extensive manoeuvring and three main engagements between 31 May to 1 June 1916 off the North Sea coast of Denmark's Jutland Peninsula. It was the largest naval battle and the only full-scale clash of battleships in The Great War. Jutland was the last major battle in naval history fought primarily by battleships.

Germany's High Seas Fleet intended to lure out, trap and destroy a portion of the British Grand Fleet, as the German naval force was insufficient to openly engage the entire British fleet. This formed part of a larger strategy to break the British blockade of Germany and to allow German naval vessels access to the Atlantic. Meanwhile, the Royal Navy pursued a strategy of engaging and destroying the High Seas Fleet, thereby keeping German naval forces contained and away from Britain and her shipping lanes, and the vital supplies required crossing the Atlantic.

The Germans planned to use a fast scouting group of five modern battlecruisers to lure Royal Navy battlecruiser squadrons into the path of the main German fleet. They additionally stationed submarines in advance across the likely routes of the British ships. However, the British learned from signal intercepts that a major fleet operation was likely.

On the afternoon of 31 May British navy ships encountered the German battlecruiser force before the Germans had expected to. In a running battle the Germans successfully drew the British vanguard into the path of their High Seas Fleet. By the time the British sighted the larger force and turned back towards the main fleet, they had lost two battlecruisers from a force of six, and four battleships. The withdrawal at the sight of the High Seas Fleet, which the British had not known were in the open sea, would reverse the course of the battle by drawing the German fleet in pursuit towards the British Grand Fleet. Between 6.30 pm that day, when the sun was lowering on the western horizon, back lighting the German forces, and nightfall at about 8.30 pm, the two fleets totalling 250 ships between them directly engaged in combat twice.

Fourteen British and eleven German ships sank, with a total of 9,823 casualties. After sunset, and throughout the night, the British manoeuvred to cut the Germans off from their base, but under the cover of darkness the Germans broke through the British lighter forces forming the rearguard and returned to port.

The British lost more ships and twice as many sailors but succeeded in containing the German fleet. The British strategy of denying Germany access to both the United Kingdom and the Atlantic did succeed, which was the long-term goal. At the end of 1916, after further unsuccessful attempts to reduce the Royal Navy's numerical advantage, the German Navy accepted that its surface ships had been contained by the Royal Navy. The Germans subsequently turned their efforts and resources to unrestricted submarine warfare and the destruction of Allied and neutral shipping. This policy would lead the American entry into the war.

During the Battle of Jutland, Midshipman Kidston aboard HMS *Orion*, the lead ship of her class of four dreadnought battleships, ran gunnery orders on open deck under direct enemy fire. He was just 17 years old when he undertook these duties. This clearly involved considerable personal danger. Entries in his personal records documenting his naval service are indicative of an exceptional leader and a highly resilient individual.

In January 1918 Kidston attended HMS *Dolphin* for submarine training. There he trained with a series of submarine depot ships (a depot ship is an auxiliary/logistics ship used as a mobile base for various craft, with limited space for crew). His report says: 'VG at taking charge, VG physically, plenty of brains. Conduct: satisfactory. Ability: excellent. Prioritises extremely well, possesses unstinting energy in everything he undertakes.' He also attended a confidential course at Cambridge University in August 1918.

Kidston then served on several British submarines, including the notorious *X1*. During North Sea trials the *X1* buried itself in the seabed as its gauges were faulty.

On 17/2/1920 his personnel records report: This officer is in need of further responsibility as a 2 I/C of a submarine. As a leader of men he has shown exceptional calmness, sympathy and tact. Inclined to be slightly cavalier probably due to a lack of responsibility. Unusually though shows exceptional organising ability.

And on 12/5/1921: Although in possession of considerable personal means, this officer has the best interests of the service at heart.

But on 17/9/1926: Convicted by civil powers for dangerously driving a motor car and failing to produce a driving licence. Fined £5 plus costs. Chief constable of Blackpool complained of his conduct towards the police and himself. The service views such reports which bring discredit on the Navy with grave displeasure.

In December 1926 he received command of *H24*, an H-class submarine built at Portsmouth by Beardmore.

On 16 October 1927 his record states that he was 'granted permission to drive a Bugatti racing boat during its trials'. Bugatti trialled an ambitious proposal to develop a semi-submersible high-powered, sleek boat designed to cross the Atlantic in fifty hours. The Kidston family are unsure if this is what Kidston was involved with, but with his submarine background and keen interest in yachting it is not unlikely.

His records shows that on 7 September 1928 he was 'retired on his own request with a gratuity of £1,200.'

Kidston then became one of the four core Bentley team drivers. The others were Woolf Barnato, Bernard Rubin and Tim Birkin. The Bentley Boys were a wealthy bunch, but Kidston was probably the wealthiest of them all. They all had apartments in the south-east corner of Grosvenor Square, which black cab drivers knew as 'Bentley Corner'.

Nicholas Foulkes in *The Bentley Era* describes what he believes motivated these characters. Like all sportsmen of that era, they were patriots who believed that after the Great War Britain was a land fit for heroes and they saw it as their duty to fulfil this heroism. These four men in particular did not have to work and lived well, but they felt an obligation to give something back to their country. They were to a degree hedonists, they raced for enjoyment, but they also represented Britain and were happy to risk their lives in doing so.

Kidston's financial means allowed him to race, shoot in Africa, fish and indulge in sport. He was a particularly keen boxer. He owned Bentleys before he drove for them.

He owned the first Bugatti in the UK. He had raced it in the 1925 Grand Prix de Provence; and he was the first person to race a new 2.0 litre Bugatti at Brooklands.

In 1925 he married beautiful debutante Nancy Soames. They had a son together, but their union was not a happy one. He promised he would give up motor racing and sold the Bugatti, but their relationship deteriorated and he began to race again.

Kidston competed at the Monte Carlo Rally, the Isle of Man TT motorcycle races, and the Shelsley Walsh Hill Climb. As a naval amateur he raced a Sunbeam motorcycle up the hill climb in Hong Kong and conducted speed trials on the sands, bringing the bike with him in his submarine which was patrolling the China Station. Kidston entered the 1929 Irish Grand Prix (Éireann Cup) at Phoenix Park but was narrowly beaten by the Alfa Romeo of former Russian Imperial Guard officer Boris Ivanowski. Kidston and Tim Birkin driving Bentleys came second and third.

The Le Mans 24-hour races in 1929 and 1930 involved Kidston racing as a 'Bentley Boy'. The 1929 race saw Bentley finish in first, second, third and fourth places with Kidston partnered with Jack Dunfee. Bentley's team ethos was not to race any faster than they needed to. With this in mind, to Dunfee's frustration they stopped and had a drink at the Café de l'Hippodrome during one of his stints. Kidston and Dunfee finished second to Barnato and Birkin. Dunfee was always considered the court jester in this group of *bon viveurs*. He was a gentleman racer who competed for pleasure. Neither he nor Kidston had financial interests in the company.

Team driver Frank Clement was an employee, and it irritated him that these self-supporting drivers lacked mechanical knowledge. Of Kidston he said, 'He was a nice chap, but would not obey orders'. One mechanic even said, 'He's the only naval officer I had to shout at.' Kidston was said amongst the Bentley crew to 'upset everybody, but be likeable all the same.'

In November 1929 Kidston was travelling from Croydon to Amsterdam in a German airliner, a Junkers G24. Twenty minutes into the flight, the pilot became disorientated in thick fog. Kidston sensed an imminent crash and assumed the safety position. He assisted fellow traveller Prince Eugen von Schaumberg-Lippe to adopt the same position. The Junkers crashed into some trees and burst into flames. Alight all over, Kidston kicked out part of the fuselage, and once free in the field into which they had crashed, doused himself on the wet grass. He re-entered the burning wreckage and dragged out the badly-burned prince, but the ferocity of the flames prevented him assisting others. Kidston fought through a mile of woodland in the dark to summon help. As he flagged a motorist down, his clothes were still smoking. The prince was too badly burned and later died. Kidston was the sole survivor. One source recounts that Kidston returned to the airfield and went up on a quick flight 'to steady his nerves' (*Canberra Times*, 8 November 1929). Then he was hospitalised and wrapped in bandages. In hospital he could only 'get a cigarette to my lips by opening a hole in the wadding.'

Le Mans in 1930 set records for the fewest entrants, only seventeen starters, the first female team, and the appearance of the supercharged Bentleys. Kidston was paired with Woolf Barnato in a works Bentley Speed

Six. They won the race, with the works Bentley team delivering a first and second placing. Team Bentley were still at the height of their powers, but it was to be their last appearance for decades, thanks to the Great Depression.

But Kidston, Barnato and Birkin were on the French Riviera by August 1930 continuing to live their very high life. Kidston had flown himself down in a Puss Moth. They were racing speed boats at Cannes, drinking champagne and cocktails, and at one point placing a vast bet on the provenance of a bottle of bootleg whiskey.

Kidston had an air of invincibility about him. He had survived being torpedoed in the Great War, the break-up of a speed boat at sea, the underwater beaching of a submarine, and while hunting in Africa he was charged by both a wounded lion and a rhino. He crashed at the 1929 Ulster TT at 95 mph, and had survived the air crash from Croydon.

Kidston found aviation as rewarding as motorsport and had begun taking flying lessons in 1927. He saw the commercial value in flying and brought glamour to it, being photographed with two pretty girls before a round England air race. Kidston believed that Britain was missing valuable opportunities in the field of air transport. The year after his Bentley/Le Mans victory he set about raising the profile of British aviation.

In April 1931 he completed a record-breaking flight from Netheravon, Wiltshire, to Cape Town, South Africa. He took six and a half days, flying his own specially adapted Lockheed Vega monoplane, averaging 131 mph. He stated in a letter, 'My object is to make people wake up. In the commercial sphere we are miles behind'. The British press reacted with great enthusiasm to his achievement.

While in South Africa he decided to conduct an aerial tour of the country, but his Vega was too big so he borrowed a Puss Moth, a plane he was familiar with, and one that could land on small local airstrips. But on the 5 May 1931 the afternoon papers in South Africa carried the following headlines:

STOP PRESS: Glen Kidston Reported Killed... aeroplane crash... visiting cards found nearby... Lieutenant Commander G.P. Glen Kidston, RN.

Kidston and his co-pilot could only be identified by the names in their shirt collars and the inscription on a signet ring given to Kidston by his wife following the birth of their son Archie. Their bodies had been smashed by the aircraft's engine on impact with the ground. The investigation concluded that the aircraft was overloaded and encountered turbulence, and that luggage had been thrown around the fuselage, damaging the plane.

After years of a loveless marriage Kidston had found love with a beautiful younger woman who would later become Margaret, Duchess of Argyll. They had been seeing each other for three months, albeit under the supervision of her mother, and on the night before he flew abroad, he dropped Margaret off and sent her a diamond Cartier watch with a note expressing his feelings. It arrived the day he died. He wrote, 'Sweetheart, I am terribly in love with you, and I didn't realise how much until I got down here.' Fifty years later Margaret said, 'I knew then as I know now that Glen Kidston was the man I should have married,' and fifty years later she still wore that Cartier watch.

Both Margaret and Barbara Cartland (also one of Kidston's lovers) claimed in their memoirs to have fainted on hearing of his death.

Another of Kidston's lovers was the Hollywood femme fatale Pola Negri. She even wrote a column about the tragedy of their lost love.

He left Nancy Soames a widow, and son Archie fatherless, but his descendants have thrived. Designer Cath Kidston is his granddaughter; he also has a nephew, classic car dealer, collector, commentator and journalist Simon Kidston.

Glen Kidston's gravestone is at St Peter's, Glasbury-on-Wye, in the Welsh borders, where he was buried on 2 June 1931. Its epitaph reads, 'Time and tide wait for no man', and it has a sundial. A memorial to him, an aluminium propeller set in stone, stands at the fateful crash site. His coffin was borne by Boy Scouts instead of gloomy pall bearers, 'Rule Britannia' was sung at his request, with his mother laying a large floral cross fabricated from the white heather that he cherished so much as a young boy.

Glen Kidston, RN, was one of three of the Bentley Boys who had survived The Great War but would not see out the 1930s to witness the Second World War.

Chapter 6

Bernard Rubin (1896-1936)

Second Lieutenant Royal Garrison Artillery in the First World War

Le Mans winner and Bentley Boy

Bernard Rubin was born on 6 December 1896 to pearl salesman Mark Rubinstein (1867-1919) and Rebecca (née Davis), of a notable Jewish family, in the suburb of Carlton, Melbourne, Australia. The family moved to London when he was 11, where they resided at 60 Elsworthy Road. Mark Rubinstein was a Lithuanian immigrant; he did with pearls what Barney Barnato had done with diamonds in South Africa.

Mark's brother Harold de Vahl Rubin was a well-known pastoral farmer, art collector and philanthropist. His brother Abraham was a wealthy entrepreneur who went down with the SS *Koombana* in March 1912 in a cyclone storm. He had just purchased the legendary Roseate Pearl for £20,000, a perfectly round, pink akoya pearl. According to legend anyone who owned it died a mysterious or violent death. The ship sank without trace and the pearl has not been seen since.

Rubin served in the OTC at University College School, Hampstead. The headmaster H.J. Spenser wrote: 'Work, conduct and progress give entire satisfaction to school authorities. Achieved standard of education fully qualifying him to hold a commission in HM Forces.'

He also served in the OTC at Queen's College, Oxford, where on 23 July 1915 W.A. Appleyard wrote: 'Mr Bernard Rubin was a pupil of mine from school to January 1916. During this whole period his conduct was unexceptionable, and he showed himself worthy in every way to hold a commission in HM Forces.'

He attained a medical fitness declaration at the Australian Military Office in Horseferry Road, Westminster, on 27 January 1916 and enlisted in St John's Wood on 5 February 1916, noting on his attestation form that he was Jewish.

He listed his preferences as Army Service Corps, Mechanical Transport Section, or the Royal Artillery.

He attended the RA OTC in Exeter from 21 February 1916 as a gunner, then moving to 'A' cadet school on 7 April, then discharged to a Special Reserve Commission on 21 June. He became a Second Lieutenant in 244 Siege Battery Royal Garrison Artillery.

During the Great War the Royal Regiment of Artillery was made up of the Royal Horse Artillery, the Royal Field Artillery and the Royal Garrison Artillery. The RGA manned the heavy guns and howitzers on the Western Front. Heavy batteries were of course a target for counter-battery fire from the Germans, as Bernard Rubin would discover to his cost. Rubin was injured and required three years of treatment before he could walk again.

It is possible that Rubin was at the Somme on 1 July 1916, but he had only completed his training ten days before the assault. It is more likely that he was training with new siege batteries in the Somme area in August 1916. In late January 1917 the battery had moved to deployment in the line at Dainville, outside Arras, where come April a major offensive would be launched. The first six weeks of the deployment would have seen Rubin take part in many supervisory duties: the selection of observation points, laying telephone lines, identification of targets, and building shelters and dugouts. Major Franklin Lushington's book *The Gambardiers* describes well what life must have been like for Bernard at the time. Lushington was CO of 244 Siege Battery.

In mid-March the Germans withdrew to the heavily fortified Hindenburg Line and the British moved their guns forward to take up the ground they had abandoned, to positions near the village of Achicourt. Rubin's guns were positioned in a quarry and they began their bombardment of the German positions on 25 March. The bombardment continued until 8 April with around two million shells being fired. The Battle of Arras commenced on Sunday, 9 April 1917, at 5.30 am and was a resounding success.

Rubin's battery continued supporting the advance of British troops for the next six weeks when a stalemate was reached. At the end of May Rubin and 244 Siege Battery were transferred to Ypres. There the battery was located in the grounds of Chateau des Trois Tours in a copse near Brielen. 244 would form part of the vast artillery bombardment of 81 Heavy Artillery Group against the German positions surrounding the Ypres salient at the start of Third Ypres that culminated in the Battle of Passchendaele. Lushington recounts how before the next assault his casualties mounted as the copse in which they were concealed was struck by German shells. Rubin's battery was reduced from six to three guns, and five out of six of the subalterns commanding the guns were wounded. One of them would have been Rubin. He was evacuated from theatre with a shrapnel wound before the Third Ypres began.

Rubin was wounded on 12 July 1917 and officially discharged from his unit the next day. He was sent through Belgium and transported from Boulogne on 27 July, arriving in Dover on the same day.

His worst injury was described as: 'Struck by a shell fragment outside the right ankle producing a compound fracture of the lateral malleolus. Surgery on 15th July to remove wound, sceptic but healed. Walking with two sticks.' But his problems did not end there:

4th September 1917

Wound – severe

Effects – still severe

Permanence – no

Recuperation period – three months

21st December 1917

Wound – severe

Effects – severe

Permanence – uncertain

20th September 1918

Wound – severe

Effects – no longer severe

Recuperation – 15 months

His records show that the wound had begun to effect his right hip with extensor muscles becoming infirm. It was three years before he could walk properly again.

Following his father's death in 1919, Rubin began purchasing properties in Australia's Northern Territory.

While still in recovery he began his interest in motorsport following a meeting with Woolf Barnato. The two became close friends and even lived together for some time.

Rubin made his driving debut at Brooklands in 1928 aged 31, partnered with Dr Dudley 'Benjy' Benjafield. They finished in sixth place. Rubin made his first appearance at the 24 Hours of Le Mans where he and Barnato won the event in a Bentley 4½ litre, despite the car being damaged during the race. He drove for Bentley at Le Mans in 1929, but his car failed after only seven laps.

It was not unknown for wine and champagne to be consumed in the pits at the time. One mechanic, Wally Hassan, said of Rubin when competing at the Irish TT of 1929: 'He was a shocker, I refused to ride with him because I had a shrewd idea that he'd be pickled.' Rubin came eighth in that race.

In August 1929 Rubin was injured when his Bentley overturned during the RAC Tourist Trophy on the first lap. The race was won by German Rudolf Caracciola who was a rising threat in his supercharged Mercedes, with Tim Birkin taking second. Rubin then turned to team management for a period, helping to support fellow Bentley Boy Tim Birkin's racing efforts with the supercharged car.

In 1933 Rubin's partnership with Birkin saw them share the wheel of an MG K3 in the Mille Miglia race in Italy, winning in their class. Birkin later drove Rubin's Maserati 3.0 litre 8C in the Tripoli Grand Prix in May 1933, coming third. This was the race in which Birkin burnt his forearms on the exhaust, dying five weeks later from blood poisoning.

In April 1934 Rubin flew to Australia in a Leopard Moth with test-pilot K.F.H. Waller to get familiar with the route and arrangements for the 'Centenary Air Race' from Mildenhall to Melbourne due to take place in October. Their return flight of 8 days, 12 hours, was not officially timed but was ten hours faster than the existing record. He entered his Bentley-green de Havilland Comet in the air race but was unable to compete due to ill health.

On 29 March 1935 in Paris, Rubin married Audrey Mary Simpson, daughter of Charles Ringham Simpson.

Bernard Rubin died in England of pulmonary tuberculosis in 1936. His body was taken back to Australia, where he is buried in Fawkner Crematorium and Memorial Park, Melbourne.

Rubin was the first of four Australians to win the 24 Hours of Le Mans. Vernon Schuppan won it in 1983, Geoff Brabham in 1993, and David Brabham in 2009, the latter two both sons of Formula One legend Sir Jack Brabham.

Chapter 7

Sir Henry Segrave (1896-1930)

Royal Warwickshire Regiment & Royal Flying Corps in the First World War

Grand Prix winner and land and water speed record breaker

Henry O'Neal de Hane Segrave was born on 22 September 1896 in Baltimore, USA, to Charles William Segrave of Wolverhampton, England, and American-born Mary Lucy (Harwood). The Segrave family can trace its heritage back to the tenth century when Thomas Segrave was lord of the village of Segrave in Leicestershire.

Henry's grandfather, Captain Henry Segrave, was a Crimean War veteran and Chief Constable of Wolverhampton – coincidentally the home of Sunbeam Cars which would become so important in Henry's life.

Captain Segrave's youngest son, Charles, chose to strike out from the family norms and joined the British Consular Service (under his Uncle William, another Crimean War veteran) where he was the assistant consul in Baltimore.

Charles Segrave made a considerable amount of money in real estate. Mary Lucy, whose father was a naval officer and grandfather the Bishop of Maryland, was described by Cyril Posthumus, Sir Henry's biographer, as 'gracious, gentle, whose soulfulness concealed a practical and far sighted outlook'. Three years into their marriage Henry was born and named after his grandfather, after some Irish forebears (O'Neal), and his paternal grandmother (de Hane). De Hane was of Huguenot descent.

Tragically in 1898 Mary was taken ill and died, accelerating Charles' desire to return to Ireland from the USA. On 4 July 1899, Charles, Henry and Mary's mother (a nurse) boarded a liner to return to the 'Old World'. They settled in 'Kiltymon', a family house in County Wicklow where Grandmother Harwood took care of Henry until another nurse/nanny was engaged and she returned to the USA.

In 1901 Charles married again, to Jessica Stone, and the new Mrs Segrave took loving care of young 'de Hane' as he is and was frequently referred to by many writers and contemporaries. They had a son, Charles Rodney, in 1904, giving young de Hane a half-brother.

In 1903 Charles senior became an official for events of the Automobile Club of Great Britain, acquired a car, a 16/20 twin-cylinder Argyll built in Glasgow, and young de Hane began his lifelong interest, perhaps obsession, with speed and the motor car. De Hane drove his first car aged 9 when the Argyll went in for repairs and the family was lent a De Dietrich car. The family chauffeur, Charles Wilson, decided to coax de Hane into the driver's seat, knowing that he had an interest in the mechanics, and soon, although he struggled to reach the pedals, he was in control and travelling at speed. A little too much speed for Wilson's liking, so he had to kill the ignition to get control. This became a regular and exciting treat. De Hane's father did not know about these little adventures until six years after his son's death.

The family moved from Wicklow to a grand house and estate in Tipperary called Belle Isle. There they engaged in many country pursuits and a large garage and workshop was constructed, much to the delight of de Hane. The car fleet expanded to include a 6 bhp Rover that de Hane would drive on the mile-long front drive with his father, always going too fast and having to be reined in. His father also purchased a speedboat to join the various boats at Belle Isle, to which de Hane also became addicted. He couldn't do anything slowly, it seemed, even cycling: he was described as passing through the local town in 'scorching' fashion dressed in grey knickerbockers and an open-necked shirt.

As well as all these other pursuits, he possessed a lavish model railway that he frequently expanded.

He was educated at home with a private tutor until the age of 10, and then sent to a prep school called Bilton Grange near Rugby, where it took him some time to settle. He was lanky, ginger-haired, short-tempered and prepared to defend himself against anyone, becoming a proficient fist fighter. He didn't mix easily and remained a loner. He found school routines stifling and very much enjoyed his holidays back in Ireland where he could regain his freedom and his passions.

At 14 he moved to Eton where a housemaster called Mr Byrne took the blue-eyed, curly-haired youth under his wing. His father had bought him a Rudge motorcycle that he rode around Ireland without fear; when he returned to Eton he took it with him, and there had his first taste of competition. With his housemaster's son Raymond Byrne and an American pupil called Deighton Simpson, they used to race around the gasometers in the cindered yard of the local gasworks. They progressed to staging their own 'TT' race across the nearby Dorney Common. Although not aboard the fastest machine, and despite his slender build, de Hane won the sprint through a mix of skill and bravery.

At Eton he joined the OTC, and had already been put down for a place with the Irish Guards. In the summer of 1913 back at home in Tipperary he was motorcycle despatch rider in exercises at a training camp with the Irish Command. He was run ragged for six days and impressed all around him with his refusal to tire until he fell asleep over his food on the last day. The officer in charge wrote to the officer commanding the Eton OTC giving him high praise. On de Hane's return he was awarded the role of 'galloper' to the corps.

On 28 June 1914 Gavrilo Princip assassinated Archduke Franz Ferdinand and his wife Sophie Chotek in Sarajevo. Five weeks later Europe was plunged into a devastating war which would be fought with industrial efficiency when it came to the slaughter of men.

In July 1914 Eton broke up for the summer holidays and de Hane made his way to the annual OTC camp at Mytchett near Aldershot. The atmosphere was electric with talk of imminent mobilisation of troops. De Hane threw himself with gusto into his role as corps galloper and, along with the rest of his unit, was disappointed when the camp was disbanded after less than a week because of the European situation.

He began a return to Ireland by motorcycle with his cousin Barry Close. They had got as far as Llangollen when they discovered that war had been declared between Britain and Germany. The cousins promptly turned around and rode back to Aldershot. Motorcycling through the night, by the time they arrived they had ridden 350 miles in 24 hours, a considerable feat considering their age, the roads and the machines. Sadly for the enthusiastic youths it was all in vain: the recruiting authorities rejected them as too young. But they advised de Hane, the older of the two, to go to the Royal Military Academy at Sandhurst as an officer cadet. He did so and passed into Sandhurst on 21 August 1914.

The fighting began immediately on the continent the day war was declared: the Germans invaded Belgium; and four days later the British Expeditionary Force arrived in France. A month later the Germans had advanced through France to the Marne River just east of Paris, and a fortnight later the opposing forces had dug into entrenched positions. From early on the casualty rate was so high that the officers' training course was reduced from two years to a frantic three months. Although de Hane was still commissioned for the Irish Guards, he studied the casualty lists and then applied to change his regiment to one that had suffered heavy losses. He passed out of training in late November 1914 and was posted to the Royal Warwickshire Regiment. He was granted leave over the Christmas period, and an opportunity to see his family, before being deployed to the continent.

It was late January 1915 when Second Lieutenant H.O.D. Segrave of the Royal Warwicks embarked with his battalion for the battlefields of northern France on a 'choppy' crossing that made him intensely seasick.

Initially based in the town of Harfleur, his first task was somewhat gruesome: the sorting of bloodstained uniforms from the front line to be sent for laundry and re-issue.

On 14 February he was posted to a mile behind the front line at Armentières with thirty men billeted at a farm with the Second Battalion the Royal Warwicks. He wrote in a letter home:

It was last night that I realised what it was like, and by Lord Harry it put the fear of God into me. We got a telephone call saying the Germans were advancing against our trenches, and so our 60 pounders got to work. I was peacefully walking home when about 350 yards away there was a blinding flash that lit up the whole place and a great roaring sort of cough that made the earth tremble, and a thing went across the sky swishing like a huge rocket.

I have never known such a terrible sound. There was no other word for it, it was terrible. It made me feel empty to my stomach. Even though they were our guns, it made me realise what this was going to be like... Then it was like Dante's Inferno let loose, the Germans sending up scores of flare shells which lit up the whole place like day. The air was trembling with the noise of the huge guns firing.

Of the German snipers he wrote:

They are A1 shots with their special rifle with telescopic sights. I held up a biscuit with a split stick and there were two shots at once, one of which bust the biscuit.

De Hane and his men, as per the description in many Great War reference books, were all too soon desensitised to shelling, mud, misery, death and the stench of decaying flesh. It is regarded that this process took roughly two weeks.

Soon after this, de Hane and his regiment were involved in the fighting at Neuve-Chapelle. It was brutal and de Hane was fortunate as a young officer to come through it leading attacks from the front with machine-gun fire cutting down hundreds of men; he saw his best friend in the regiment fall right in front of him. He was detailed to take an enemy trench with a group of sixty men; he achieved his objective but with only fourteen of them left. He was then ordered to fall back to the start line, which he found infuriating: 'This was the close of the 13th, and one of the unluckiest days I have lived through.'

Some of the wounded from Neuve-Chapelle were sent to hospital in Dublin and de Hane asked his father Charles to look them up. Charles did exactly that and took some of them out for a drive. He said one of the corporals 'gave me a great account of de Hane's keenness and bravery. I felt awfully bucked. He said they named him "the lion's cub" and the men would follow him anywhere, and that he was very popular.'

After a period of leave de Hane returned to the French–Belgian border and was thrown into the actions around the Second Battle of Ypres which spanned April into May 1915. He was then a machine-gun officer in charge of seven guns. He wrote to his parents about his experiences at Aubers:

The 7th and 8th divisions attacked but the enemy must have got wind of it and they mowed us down like the wind; it was the most awful and ghastly murder I have ever seen. The 8th left 9,000 dead between our lines… I myself had the most extraordinary luck with my guns; we made use of every bit of cover and never lost one man. I had a bullet pass along my wrist and go out after passing through about three inches of skin. The colonel wanted me returned as wounded but I didn't think it was bad enough.

But his luck would run out a few days later when he was seriously injured by an enemy bullet. He wrote to his parents:

I got hit around 10.30am on May 16th. We had just penetrated the German lines and forced them back over a mile. I had the deuce of a time getting back. I was so weak I could only crawl a few hundred yards at a time and then rest and go on again. When I did get to the dressing station, I presented a grizzly sight, my back, chest and face were all bluggy! The chap shot me from about four yards off. He came for me with a bayonet; my revolver was clogged with mud, jammed and useless, and I had thrown it away long before. All I had was a machine gun ammunition belt which I threw at him as hard as I could. It got him in the chest and stopped him. And then he put up his rifle and pulled the trigger. I just ducked in time and the bullet went through my left shoulder and passed out at the bottom of the shoulder blade.

The records show that he was injured at Festubert. He was evacuated from the front line on the same day, and the next day (17 May) he was repatriated to Britain on the *St Andrew*.

He was hospitalised at the King Edward VII near Harley Street. His parents were informed and Charles came to see him straight away. By good fortune, as x-rays confirmed, the shot had not damaged any bone. After five days, although weak, he was well enough to be discharged, and he returned to Belle Isle with his father to recuperate. In a month he was in front of a medical board, but they were dissatisfied with the progress of the healing of his shoulder muscles and he was signed off for another two months.

It was then that he bought his first car and went on a driving tour of the UK with his father, visiting his old schools, and aerodromes: in the trenches he had often looked up in wonder at the planes of the Royal Flying Corps passing overhead. At his next visit to the medical board he was passed fit for home service and de Hane was posted to the 33rd Division based at Tidworth. He immediately applied to join the RFC, but the army authorities were reluctant to transfer a battle-experienced infantry officer. Frustrating weeks went by and he applied again. His division were due to be transferred to the Dardanelles (infamous for the Gallipoli campaign). But on 15 October 1915 he received a telegram ordering Second Lieutenant H.O.D. Segrave to report to the RFC flying school at Upavon in Wiltshire.

De Hane achieved his flying certificate, completing three and half hours of dual instruction and two and half hours of solo flying, in a Fairman Longhorn, a fragile canvas and wood flying contraption whose 75 bhp engine struggled to propel it at 60 mph. However, this was insufficient to meet the standards set by the Royal Aero Club, so he had to put in additional hours on a variety of other aircraft. He gained his wings as an RFC pilot on 1 January 1916. Additionally he was promoted to full or first lieutenant.

He was posted to Castle Bromwich where he was tasked with ferrying and testing aircraft, and much of his non-combat flying in the UK would prove almost as dangerous as being at the front. He wrote:

Curse these rotten machines, the Arrol-Johnston people are turning out, and 'Gotte Strafe' the Beardmore engines. At 5,000 feet over Kineton near Banbury, first a control wire broke and then immediately afterwards two rocker arms broke clean in half and so the engine just stopped. The machine nose-dived at once and I just righted her in time and landed without breaking a single thing!

Having repaired the plane, the next morning de Hane took off and three more rockers broke, bringing him down. But he had several spares, and got the plane back to Netheravon. He then got the train to Birmingham where he met his parents and they went to the theatre together. They emerged into a Zeppelin raid, and so de Hane dashed off to Castle Bromwich airfield in the hope of getting airborne and shooting down one of these German airships. But by the time he was ready to take off, the Zeppelins had gone.

De Hane was then transferred to an RFC scouting squadron (29th Squadron, RFC) based in Netheravon, which delighted him no end as he would be able to fly de Havilland DH2s equipped with single machine guns. Their job was to be escort and attack aircraft in France, and he threw himself into mastering this role with gusto.

Several weeks of ferrying aircraft work ensued before the squadron was posted to France. He flew his first patrol on 21 April 1916, and on his third patrol days later he was attacked by a Fokker that dived on him from behind with a short burst of fire before heading for the German lines. De Hane gave chase letting off fifty rounds, but his DH2 could not catch his adversary.

On 1 May de Hane shot down a two seater Aviatek artillery observation plane reconnoitring Ypres. Five weeks later he was shot down by another such plane.

A replacement DH2 did not bring him much confidence: it was mechanically inferior, and despite it being inspected and serviced with the same care as his last, it was slower. To top it all, the guns jammed when he was closing in on a kill with a German Albatross scout and he was forced to disengage.

He was promoted to captain or flight commander on 1 July 1916 and issued with a new fighter aircraft called the FE8 Scout. It could climb to 10,000 feet, fly at 90 mph, and was mechanically superior to the Fokkers; at this time it was only one of two such aircraft deployed to France.

Three days later he was shot down by anti-aircraft fire. A shell struck him at 7,000 feet, shattering the plane's controls. He managed somehow to return to the aerodrome at Abeele, but hitting soft ground the plane flipped onto its back leaving de Hane hanging from the cockpit with a blow to his head and a shattered left ankle joint. On 10 July he was back in hospital in London undergoing treatment for a complex fracture that was so serious that some even advocated amputation.

He knew his flying days were over and with this realisation came a relaxation of his mental state with the pressure gone from being an active RFC pilot. A relaxed 19-year-old began to return, but his boyish outlook on life had long gone, with war forcing mental and physical maturity upon him. He had also developed an incredible sense of judgement from a deep consideration of facts which avoided rash and precipitous decisions, a quality that would prove invaluable in motor racing.

Great War records of the RFC indicate de Hane as being a satisfactory and adequate pilot but no further praise or description beyond that. In his later years he was self-deprecating, describing himself as a 'rotten pilot' and 'I wasn't so bad once I was up, but I always seemed to make a mess of landing.'

Six weeks after his crash landing he was recuperating back at Belle Isle on crutches. However, his father was concerned at his drawn look and called the family doctor who determined that he needed further treatment and he was sent back to London for the fitting of a special support.

After two months he was still listless; he didn't wish to shoot as he had seen enough of that at the front, and fishing and boating had also lost its spark. His father sent him to England to buy himself a car and he returned with an 'Itala' sporting tourer with 120 bhp and a top speed of 90 mph. He used it to drive a family friend, Colonel Carr Ellison, on a tour of the West of Ireland.

Soon he was returned to duty with the RFC, but with his ankle still not fully healed he was signed off for 'sedentary work only' and worked at the War Office in London. He brought his Itala car with him. In his work he turned out to have a great organisational talent and was described as 'a demon for work'. His ferrying work and combat flying in France proved valuable, as one of his duties was to lecture RFC personnel.

During this time he began dating a musical comedy actress called Doris Stocker and his father came to work in London for the Ministry of Munitions. Problems with de Hane's ankle returned and the medical board recommended amputation, but he found a skilled orthopaedic surgeon who removed some small bones and replaced them with silver plates. The surgeon could not have known this foot would go on to receive quite a hammering from clutch pedal operation in his racing and land-speed-record-breaking career.

In May 1917 de Hane was back in France for a third time at the RFC HQ on executive duties. After two months he returned to London and on 4 October he and Doris married at the Church of St Cyprian in Dorset Square. They spent a honeymoon in Somerset and Scotland and, unlike the spouses of many other drivers, Doris would enthusiastically support his participation in motorsport. They settled in No 6 St Andrew's Mansions (Mayfair 5069 if telephoning!) just off Baker Street. He returned to work at the war office and presented Doris with a bulldog puppy called Laddie.

In April 1918 the RFC and the Royal Naval Air Service were combined to form the RAF and de Hane was recommended to work as a staff officer with the Secretary of State for War. Now 21, he became private secretary to Sir Henry Norman, a member of the Air Council who wrote a glowing letter of praise thanking de Hane for his service. This led to his appointment as Technical Secretary to the Council.

He was sent to the USA as part of a mission to help the Americans establish their military aviation; this meant a trip back to the country of his birth and promotion to major. He departed on 18 June 1918, accompanied by Doris and Laddie, on the *Empress of Britain*. Painted in wartime camouflage it formed up in a convoy, escorted by Royal Navy destroyers and cruisers for protection, and zigzagged across the Atlantic Ocean bound for Nova Scotia. The passage was tense; life preservers were to be worn at all times, frequent lifeboat drills were practised, and the *Empress* was particularly slow. Doris was advised, 'If there's trouble don't go for the lifeboats, grab a deckchair and throw that in the sea and dive in to use that to float.' A cargo vessel of 10,000 tons travelling abreast of the *Empress* was hit by a torpedo and sunk in 23 minutes. But they got there. A train journey followed via New York, Baltimore (where de Hane visited family) and on to Washington where the British aviation mission was based. After the privations of Britain at war, the wonderland of plenty that was America was a bright relief.

Major and Mrs Segrave took an apartment nearby and de Hane's enthusiastic affability won over those he worked with, coupled with his extensive knowledge and experience. He travelled frequently to New York for work and encountered a man called Bill Bruce-Brown, who was the brother of late racing driver David Bruce-Brown. Their conversation included motor racing. Later de Hane read in the press of a race meeting at nearby Sheepshead Bay where the winning driver had achieved an averaged 110 mph. He went to the track and sought permission to drive himself, which he was granted. After a sighting lap he drove as hard as he could in a 60 bhp Apperson car he had bought for commuting and achieved a lap speed of 82 mph, to his great personal satisfaction.

November 1918 saw the end of the Great War and he, Doris, Laddie and the car returned, with some difficulty as they were not priority passengers, to the UK. His powers to charm and persuasion had not deserted him. He gained passage for them and the car only a month after the signing of the truce. On arrival back at their London Dorset Street address he sought demobilisation at his earliest opportunity.

In a couple of months he was a civilian and he invested in the Cubitt Car Company and in a car dealership in Knightsbridge run by fellow veteran Captain Alistair Miller. Miller possessed two pre-war Opel Grand Prix 4½ litre cars which fired de Hane's imagination. He persuaded Miller to get them to Brooklands for him to try on the track.

He also made the acquaintance of Louis Coatalen (who got Eddie Rickenbacker released from his confinement aboard a ship in 1916) who was a director at the Sunbeam Motor Company, and would soon oversee the amalgamation of Sunbeam with Talbot and Darracq to form S-T-D. De Hane asked Coatalen for a chance to drive for his team. Coatalen had too many approaches from want-to-be racing drivers: 'Another hopeful who thinks he can just climb into a racing car and press the pedals hard.' He told de Hane he needed more experience and his claim of racing at Sheepshead in the USA and 'on other tracks like that' just didn't cut it.

Miller and de Hane went to Brooklands with the Opels, and the would-be racer lapped the outer ring at 90 mph. It was apparent he could handle a car with finesse, being particularly adept at smooth and accurate use of the gearbox. His 'feel' for the car and sympathetic driving action would, as it does today, provide greater longevity to the reliable performance of a car. There were no synchromesh gear boxes in those days, smoothness was achieved by feel, precise timing and 'ear', and de Hane took this skill to a fine art. De Hane was also fastidious in how he turned himself out – and the car – pouring scorn on any form of shabbiness.

He entered his first meeting at Brooklands on Whitsunday 1920. In his first race he got into second place having passed Captain Malcolm Campbell, but lost a tyre as he closed in on the leader. He was able to drive the car back to the pits. In his second race, the last of the day, he was in a field that included fellow motorsports' military heroes Woolf Barnato and Tim Birkin. The 'scratch man' de Hane Segrave passed the entire field and won the race. This was only his second entry. The press praised his skill at saving the car after the tyre incident more than the win, but he knew it was the exposure he needed to get the attention of Coatalen at Sunbeam. Coatalen had in fact witnessed the spectacle first-hand.

At a sprint event in July 1920 on the promenade at Southend in Essex *The Motor* magazine said: 'One of the star turns of the day was Major Segrave who whipped away from the line like a startled hare and shot up the track at a fine speed.'

At the August bank holiday meeting at Brooklands in 1920 de Hane asked Coatalen if he could drive his car again but received another discouragingly negative response. At the meeting de Hane set off in the short handicap race in a re-bodied Opel. He made his usual efficient smooth start, passed John Duff and eventually the others in the field, and crossed the line at 89 mph winning by eight feet. He won his next race too, and then a month later, still at Brooklands, he placed two seconds, to Count Zborowski and Malcolm Campbell, both in superior machinery. By the end of the Brooklands season, de Hane had achieved three firsts, two seconds, three thirds and a fifth. In October he approached Coatalen, now of S-T-D (Sunbeam-Talbot-Darracq), for the 1921 season. The 'patron' was still difficult: 'You have shown you can race in a straight line, but road racing is much more than that, you must know how to corner fast, gear change and you must be able to do that and more for several hours for grand prix. Do you think you can do that?'

'Yes,' said de Hane, 'I am fit, give me a try, give me the chance.' Coatalen gazed at the persistent young man before him, tall, alert and confident. S-T-D needed drivers for their ambitious plans and the pool of the old school drivers was thinning out. Racing was after all a young man's game. The patron shrugged: 'Perhaps, we will see.'

In 1920, now 24, de Hane moved with his wife to a house in St John's Wood (Elm Tree Road). He heard that Coatalen had begun to select drivers for the year and drove to Sunbeam in Wolverhampton. The Frenchman was in an affable mood: de Hane got a trial seat to race at the Le Mans Grand Prix; but he would have to meet his own expenses and pay for any damage to the car.

De Hane then sold his share in Alistair Miller's motor business (coming out £1,500 down) and went to work for KLG spark plugs. Through the Jarrett & Lett showroom in Conduit Street he became aware of a Bugatti for sale that had won the GP des Voiturettes at Le Mans that year. He secured a loan and went to the Bugatti works at Molsheim to collect it, where he was hosted by Ettore Bugatti. On his way home he visited Louis Coatalen whose yacht was moored in Rouen. He told him he might go and try out his new Bugatti on the Le Mans circuit. Coatalen urged caution but was happy for him to practice his road driving ready for the Grand Prix.

De Hane went to Le Mans in February 1921 with the other Sunbeam drivers Réné Thomas and Andre Boillot. They drove the public road circuit where they had to negotiate farm carts, slow cars and lorries as they lapped. Before the Grand Prix event de Hane drove in various races using both his Bugatti and Sunbeams. *The Autocar* noted of one: 'Major Segrave's driving was superb, his cornering wonderfully well-judged and his acceleration after the last corner terrific.'

Henry Segrave took his personal preparation seriously, becoming physically fit for what would be a 325-mile race. Then S-T-D decided to withdraw their cars. De Hane sought the help of K.L. Guinness, owner of the spark plug company and his closest friend. They confronted the managing director of S-T-D who relented and allowed the entry of four of the original seven cars.

Thirteen cars began the race on 25 June 1921, including the far superior Duesenbergs. On lapping de Hane at one point, a Duesenberg threw up a rock that crashed through de Hane's stone guard, ricocheted from the steering wheel and hit his riding mechanic, Moricceau, in the face, gashing him and knocking him out for five miles. But he recovered, and during the race the pair had to deal with an oil leak, a breakdown of the ignition timing, and changing fourteen tyres. By the end of the race the eight-cylinder car was running on six and they finished ninth and last. But they did finish, and *The Autocar* said: 'Driving with great skill and coolness between intervals of trouble with tyres and ignition, he may be said to have surpassed the

labours of Hercules and, as he intended, drove to an honourable finish.'
Louis Coatalen now engaged de Hane full time.

Segrave's first outing as a team driver was the Voiturettes GP at Le Mans
in which he finished third in a 1,500cc Talbot-Darracq behind his other
teammates. The next outing was in October 1921 at Brooklands in another
1,500cc race, with the S-T-D team again taking the podium positions, but
this time de Hane was the winner. By the end of the season he had gone from
being an unknown driver to a rising star.

The 1922 season started well for de Hane, with a second and third place at
the Easter meeting at Brooklands in large capacity cars. At the royal meeting
with the future George VI as patron de Hane took a win and another second.

The next event was on the TT course on the Isle of Man. De Hane spent
a week obsessively preparing himself for the race: if he was not driving the
course he was talking about it. It paid off as he posted the fastest practice lap.

Thursday, 22 June 1922, was wet. Setting off at timed intervals de Hane
was third away from the line behind a Vauxhall and a Bentley. He settled into
his drive and then upped his pace, with his hallmark supersmooth driving
paying dividends in braking, deceleration and acceleration. The pouring rain
was uncomfortable in the open car with no screen, and although his mechanic
Paul Dutoit was getting its full force in his face, he watched de Hane's driving
with admiration. Halfway round the 37¾ mile course they had caught and
passed the Vauxhall and the Bentley. He completed the first lap in 39 minutes
15 seconds and was two minutes faster than anyone else, and the fastest of
the day. On lap three he was still two minutes ahead, but the fairytale wasn't
to last: one of the magnetos failed and the car came to a halt. They limped
on with four cylinders but it didn't have the power to make it up the inclines
and de Hane and Dutoit were forced to abandon the race. But they did get
the trophy for the fastest lap.

At the next event, the Strasbourg Grand Prix, the fastest cars in practice
were the Fiats. The Sunbeams were unlikely to trouble them. Not long into
the race de Hane was the only Sunbeam left, and was holding fourth position
when a piston blew. His race was over. In the race the rear axle failed on two
of the Fiats, one of which caused a fatal accident. De Hane's own retirement
had come as a slight relief as during a refuelling stop his seat had been doused
in petrol and he had suffered chemical burns.

The rest of the season saw de Hane as a regular podium finisher, with a
third place in mid-September at the Le Mans GP des Voiturettes, two wins

at Brooklands in late September in the 5.0 litre and 2.0 litre classes, and a second in the Coppa Florio in Italy in November.

The next season, 1923, is his most famous. Louis Coatalen enticed a key Fiat engineer to come to Sunbeam. He needed a new 2.0 litre car to be ready for the Tours GP in France on 2 July. Vincenzo Bertarione chose a six-cylinder engine resembling the power plants in the dominant Fiats of the previous year. By June they were being tested by the team's star drivers, which included de Hane. Once at Tours he practiced assiduously. Dutoit timed him in specific parts of the track and then compared his pace to others. They also practiced pit drills.

But when the Fiats turned up they created another stir: they were now eight cylinders instead of six. Making a mighty roar, their fastest driver lapped 34 seconds quicker than de Hane, the fastest of the Sunbeams. It wasn't just the eight cylinders, the Fiats also had superchargers fitted, which forced the fuel-air mixture into the engine instead of allowing the compression sequence to just suck it in, thus creating a bigger 'bang' and increasing the power.

At 8 am on 2 July seventeen cars began a rolling start. De Hane found himself in a steady sixth, but after eight laps the leading Fiat broke down placing fellow Sunbeam driver and close friend K.L. Guinness into the lead. But de Hane's clutch began to slip and by lap fifteen the Fiats were leading; Guinness had lost the lead with a pitstop. Suddenly in de Hane's car there was a loud crack and the clutch suddenly worked perfectly. A bolt designed to control the rearward pedal movement was in fact restricting its movement. By luck it snapped off allowing full travel of the clutch pedal. One of the Sunbeams faltered in the pits with a seized fuel filler cap and de Hane found himself in second place behind the lead Fiat of factory driver Carlo Salamano. Then, two kilometres from the pits, Salamano's Fiat stopped. De Hane passed the stricken car with mechanic Dutoit shouting, 'It's broken down! We're leading!' In fact it had run out of fuel. With two laps to go, another Sunbeam was second (Albert Divo's – Guinness had dropped from third to fourth with mechanical issues). Segrave crossed the finishing line first, and in doing so became the first ever British driver to win the French Grand Prix; and he had done so in a British car. Much celebration took place over the following days. De Hane then drove his car from Tours back to London, being feted by the French population and assisted by gendarmes along the way.

In the rest of 1923 he took part in only two events – the speed trials and the Grand Prix in Boulogne – but he did win them.

He had become a household name: if police officers caught motorists speeding they often used to say, 'Who do you think you are, Major Segrave?'

In 1924-26 he won four GPs, two hill climbs and two speed trials driving for S-T-D. He didn't win the 1924 French GP, he came fifth, but he did race against Robert Benoist who finished third; and he crossed paths with Enzo Ferrari at the event.

In 1924 de Hane adopted the wearing of a protective helmet. He and 'Sammy' Davis of Bentley had developed the idea together. The 'bone dome' made its first appearance at Brooklands, smartly finished in white and receiving much comment.

Perhaps his greatest race during this period was the 1924 Spanish Grand Prix at St Sebastian. With the rest of the Sunbeam team he left for the Lasarte circuit in late September. It was going to be a battle between Italy (Diatto), Germany (Mercedes), France (Delage & Bugatti), and of course Britain. The race was on an eleven-mile circuit over a distance of 386 miles. The drivers included Robert Benoist, Albert Divo, and de Hane's good friend and teammate Kenelm Guinness. Sadly, Guinness had a crash that seriously injured him and killed his riding mechanic. De Hane's car was the quick and efficient 2.0 litre, six-cylinder supercharged Sunbeam. He won the race in pouring rain by a minute and half. He was presented to Queen Victoria Eugenie of Spain and received the King of Spain's Trophy. *The Excelsior* of Bilbao said: 'Segrave won with a master hand. His lap chart revealed remarkable regularity proving his scientific driving and knowledge of motor racing. Segrave seemed to have in his head from start to finish a timetable, gave his car every kindness and, we repeat, won with a master hand! He is el Maestro Completo.'

As already noted, Segrave had already competed with several other 'Motorsport's Military Heroes'. In 1925 when he won the Grand Prix de Provence he was initially given a run for his money in a Bugatti driven by Lieutenant Commander Glen Kidston which eventually developed a mis-fire. He had S.C.H. 'Sammy' Davis as a team-mate at Le Mans for Sunbeam, with John Duff having won for Bentley the year before and driving again this season. Robert Benoist was also a rival in the 1925-26 seasons driving for Delage.

In 1926 de Hane took his last GP win at the Miramas circuit in France. His driving was observed to be pin-point accurate and smooth. He was now renowned as one of the best cornerers in the world, keeping perfect poise, stability and balance.

The 1926 season saw the first British GP at Brooklands. Segrave failed to finish due to a breakdown but set the fastest lap. Setting speed records was to be the next phase of his career.

At the end of that season Sunbeam had set out to build a 1,000bhp car: a twin aero-engine (two 12-cylinder Matabele engines) 45 litre car christened *Mystery*.

In March 1926 Segrave had driven a 4.0 litre Sunbeam to a record speed at the time of 152 mph on a beach at Southport. He was looking to exceed 200 mph and to do so it was calculated he would need 3½ miles to accelerate and 2 miles to decelerate. Nowhere in the UK could offer this, but Daytona Beach in Florida could with its 20-mile stretch. The endeavour required all of de Hane's organising skills to secure the backing, the mechanics, permissions in the USA, and the cooperation of the American Automobile Association to recognise the attempt.

Dunlop constructed tyres that could withstand the stresses of a three-ton 23-foot-long car accelerating to and travelling at 200 mph or more. The drive chain could prove a hazard: one had broken and hit a driver called Parry Thomas in the head, killing him at Pendine Sands. After this accident the drive chain on de Hane's car was boxed in with a guard plate.

For de Hane there were 28 instruments to be monitored in the cockpit, including 4 rev counters, 6 oil pressure gauges and 3 temperature gauges. He watched the car run up on a test rig and commented, 'I think I watched the monster like a child would have done. This was something more gigantic than anything I had yet dreamed of. It is the only time I have stood in front of a car and doubted my ability to control it.'

The team sailed to the USA in early March, and were soon practising and refining the car. On Tuesday, 29 March 1927, in front of a crowd of 30,000 along a nine-mile section of Daytona Beach, de Hane took his chance to enter the history books as the fastest man on land. Beginning his runs at 9.30 am ('a gentleman's hour'), the area had been cleared for safety by police, two cavalry squadrons, marshals and AAA officials. Cameramen were in place, and officials to time/record/judge. Twelve-foot marker poles with three-foot square flags were in place to mark the officially measured distance.

His first test run had him fighting for control with sidewinds, and he found that the nine-mile stretch was not enough to slow down the car with its brakes alone; he used some shallow water formed by sandbanks to shave off some speed. The roar of the engine starting and under acceleration was by all accounts incredible. On the return run he again battled with sidewinds, leaving his arms aching.

But he did it: he hit 203 mph, breaking Malcolm Campbell's record by 28 mph. He wanted to go out again as he felt he could go faster, but his associates advised him not to. He was feted during the rest of his time in America and entertained by John D. Rockefeller and Commodore Garfield 'Gar' Wood, America's 'Segrave of the water'. He was so inspired by this meeting that he immediately ordered two racing boat hulls.

On return to Britain, de Hane was celebrated, and the Sunbeam *Mystery* went on display in Selfridges where it was seen by thousands of people.

In April 1927 de Hane announced that he would retire from motor racing at the end of the season and take up motorboat racing, to 'do for the British motorboat what I have done for the British car'.

In the meantime he became a director of Portland Cement with a salary rumoured to be £5,000 per year. They insisted there would be no more motor racing and de Hane said, 'I have raced for eight years and already exceeded my allotted span of luck. I shall tempt fate no longer.' But soon he managed to convince the directors to support a new land speed record, not only with his participation but by also providing sponsorship. The Irving-Napier car, *Golden Arrow*, was manufactured at KLG Spark Plugs' Robin Hood works at Putney Vale.

At this time de Hane was also making a name for himself as a powerboat racer, winning seven races, and he decided on another attempt at the water speed record. The boat, named *Miss England*, was fitted with the same 900 bhp Napier Lion twelve-cylinder engine as the *Golden Arrow*, and the headlines read 'Double Death Gamble'.

In 1928 Malcolm Campbell had broken de Hane's land speed record in *Bluebird* achieving 206.95 mph. Soon after, American Ray Keech upped the record marginally to 207.5 mph. On 9 February 1929 de Hane and his crew were in Florida with *Golden Arrow*.

After one practice run getting the car up to 180 mph the weather closed in. After fourteen days the conditions were still not perfect but de Hane could wait no longer. The American team were on standby with a new 'pilot', Lee Bible, to snatch back the record immediately if de Hane took it. De Hane turned up in spotless white overalls in front of a crowd of 100–120,000 and greeted the chief timekeeper and the AAA officials. Then, after a test run and a tyre change, Major H.O.D. Segrave smashed the record, achieving 231.2 mph. The next day the US team made their attempt to regain the record in *White Triplex*. It ended in disaster. Bible left his braking till too late and lost control, killing a photographer; then the car overturned and Bible was thrown out and killed. De Hane witnessed this and abandoned any further idea of such ventures. *Golden Arrow* came back to the UK where it now sits on display at the motor museum at Beaulieu.

On his return to Europe he received a hero's welcome in Le Havre, Southampton, and eventually London where a procession of sixty cars took him to the Berkeley Hotel. There he was entertained by the Society of Motor Manufacturers and Traders.

On Saturday, 27 May 1929, at Craigweil House in Bognor Regis where the king was convalescing, Segrave became Major Sir Henry Segrave. After a lunch with Queen Mary, they left via the tradesman's entrance to avoid the press. Then de Hane went on a speaking tour. His delivery was always well received, raising the comment, 'That man should go into politics, he could be the prime minister!' But this was not a path that interested him. Later that year he won a boat event at the Venice Lido where he also set a speed record for a 'single engine hydroplane'.

In 1930, Segrave secured the use of Lake Windemere to attempt a new water speed record in his latest boat, *Miss England II*. On the way to Lake Windermere on one of his preparatory trips he stopped at the workshops of his old friend 'Tim' Birkin in Welwyn Garden City. Birkin invited Segrave to drive one of his supercharged 'blower' Bentleys that year at Le Mans.

'Not on your life,' replied Segrave, 'But you could come and be my riding mechanic on the lake?'

'Not on your life!' replied Birkin. Neither of them would see the decade out.

On 1 June the Segraves drove to Windermere in their Rolls-Royce Phantom. During a course inspection de Hane felt a pang of nostalgia as they passed Belle Isle in the centre of the lake – the name of his childhood home in Tipperary. He had not been back there for many years. The banks around Bowness Bay were filled with people by 8 am on Thursday, 5 June, ready to witness this latest daredevil adventure, but they were to be disappointed: he slowed to avoid engulfing other boats with his wash and as a result his engine overheated. Five days later he took *Miss England II* out in the evening with no crowds. They achieved an unverified 107 mph and a propeller broke. Propellers were to prove *Miss England II*'s weak point: the metallurgy of the day could not produce a strong enough blade. A series of blades of different materials were tried, on one occasion achieving 101.9 mph, again unverified.

On Friday, 13 June, de Hane declared that he would try an official run the next day. It was to be his last chance as the official timekeepers had to go to the Isle of Man to officiate at TT races. Thousands again turned out to watch. The weather was glorious at 1.15 pm as *Miss England II* was towed from her shed to save stress on her propellers.

The first outward run went smoothly at record pace and Sir Henry turned *Miss England II* around for a return leg at slightly increased engine speed. Michael Wilcocks, the riding engineer, later commented on how well the boat was running with the hull just touching the water. Suddenly a thud was heard from the front of the hull. The boat swerved to port, de Hane straightened it then it swerved to starboard, he then straightened it again, but then the bow rose into the air and *Miss England II* flipped over.

Boats rushed to the scene and lifted Segrave and Wilcocks from the water. The third crew member Vic Halliwell, from Rolls-Royce and the engine specialist, had died instantly and was recovered later. Segrave was taken to a house on the west side of the lake. His injuries were serious: a head injury, both his arms and some ribs broken, a leg crushed. Lady Segrave was with him and gave him the news that he had broken the record; the speed was later given as 98.76 mph. Segrave died a little later, remaining conscious for all but his last two minutes. It is widely held, and Michael Wilcocks was adamant about it, that had de Hane been alone he could have jumped clear as the boat began to lose a safe path. But he fought it to try to save them all and not abandon anyone.

When the wreck of *Miss England II* was raised from the lake two weeks later, a rupture was discovered in the hull. The official explanation suggested this was the result of hitting a branch floating on the lake's surface; others have suggested that the hull's design may have been flawed. The coroner recorded a verdict of accidental death. De Hane had declined a life jacket as only one of the three ordered had been delivered and he refused to wear one if there weren't enough for all of the crew. It is unlikely anyway that it would have saved him or Halliwell. In 1930 the Segrave Trophy was established in tribute for outstanding British accomplishments in land, sea, air, or water transport.

Just Lady Doris, Sir Henry's parents, and Lord Wakefield of Portland Cement, financier of the *Miss England II* project, attended a private funeral at Golders Green Crematorium. A public memorial service was conducted at the same time in St Margaret's Church, Westminster. The church was full, with two hundred more people standing outside. Wreaths were placed at the cenotaph in Whitehall. Later that year de Hane's ashes were scattered from a Segrave Meteor aircraft (another project in which he had been involved) over the playing fields of Eton.

The loss of Major Sir Henry O'Neal de Hane Segrave is difficult to calculate with its effect for the era. For sheer versatility of achievement, he had no peer with his victories in car racing, boat racing and land speed records. As tributes poured in from around the world, Britain mourned the loss of a true national hero.

Chapter 8

Eddie Rickenbacker (1890-1973)

US Army Air Service in the First World War

Indianapolis 500 Driver

Congressional Medal of Honour recipient

Edward Vernon Rickenbacker was born on 8 October 1890 to Swiss-German immigrants Wilhelm and Liezl Rickenbacker in Livingston Avenue, Columbus, Ohio. They were responsible for installing a strong work ethic and love for his native country from an early age. His boyhood home was once described as follows: 'In around 1893 or 1895 William Rickenbacker built the first part of a simple L shaped gable-roofed dwelling. Initially the house consisted of two downstairs and two attic rooms.' It was while living here that Eddie developed his interest in cars, planes and mechanics, and it would be Eddie who would eventually pay the mortgage off on the house.

The Rickenbackers (the name is anglicised from Richenbacher) were not a wealthy family. In the house they built they had no running water or electricity. They lived in a largely rural, agrarian community, with father William being a practical-minded disciplinarian, and mother Elizabeth a deeply religious woman. Eddie remained close to his mother right up to her death in 1946.

As a child Eddie loved to deconstruct and reconstruct things, under the mantra from his father that 'a machine has to have a purpose'. Eddie was no angel: he was smoking by the age of 5 and headed a gang of young rogues known as the Horsehead Gang. Aged 8 he led the gang in a kind of soap-box cart down a slide into a deep gravel pit. It flipped onto its side, landing on him and cutting his leg to the bone. He also tried to 'fly' a bicycle outfitted with an umbrella off his friend's barn roof.

On the other hand, he helped in the family garden, harvesting potatoes, cabbages, and turnips, and cared for the animals: chickens, goats and pigs. He brought in money by delivering papers, setting up pins at the bowling alley, and selling scavenged goods to the junk man. He gave most of his nickels to his mother, but spent some on Bull Durham tobacco. He had picked up the smoking habit from his older brother Bill.

Eddie was a hard worker, streetwise and tough, but he was accident-prone. In his autobiography he recounts numerous scrapes from his early years. Once he walked into the path of a horse-drawn streetcar, and in another incident fell twelve feet into an open drain. Early in his school career, he ran back into his burning school building to retrieve his winter coat, nearly paying for it with his life. He fell out of a walnut tree and was knocked unconscious. His brother rescued him from the path of a passing coal car not once but twice. Sixty years later when writing his autobiography, he found significance in these close calls. He believed that God had repeatedly saved him for a higher purpose. He calculated that altogether in his life he had dodged death on around 135 occasions.

Mother Elizabeth on Eddie: 'In boyhood and in manhood thought and action were inseparable, and his father had installed a sense of action over procrastination. He was a mischievous boy, but never a bad boy, and his curiosity for mechanics usually kept him indoors and out of trouble.'

Eddie's childhood came to a sudden halt not long before his 14th birthday when his father died. On a hot July day, an African-American man named William Gaines asked for handouts from William Rickenbacker's sidewalk crew during their lunch break. Rickenbacker objected, 'If I had any dinner to share with any person I would share it with my children,' and foolishly wouldn't let the matter drop. Gaines struck him over the head with a spirit level; he later claimed it was in self-defence. William Rickenbacker was in a coma for six weeks before his death on 26 August 1904. Gaines was convicted of manslaughter and sentenced to ten years in prison. Eddie Rickenbacker's biographer David Lewis believed that the relatively lenient sentence suggests that Rickenbacker did in fact threaten Gaines.

Eddie decided it was up to him to support the family. Despite his older brother Bill and older sister Mary both working, he dropped out of school to enter full time work. He began, having lied about his age, at the Federal Glass Factory, then went on to the Buckeye Steel Casting Company. From there he worked in a brewery, as a monumental mason, and then became an apprentice with the Pennsylvania Railway. He worked at eight different jobs during the next two years. At the same time he taught himself as much as he could. While working at the Oscar Lear Automobile Company on the corner of Fourth and Gay streets in Columbus he enrolled in a correspondence course in engineering.

In 1906, aged 16, he went to work for a racing driver and engineer called Lee Frayer, head of the Frayer-Miller Automobile Company. Frayer took Rickenbacker under his wing, giving him more responsibility in the workshop with each passing week. Two months later, when it came time to compete in the 1906 Vanderbilt Cup race, Frayer took Eddie to New York to be his riding mechanic. But accidents cut short their two practice runs on the 29.7 mile road course, an overheated engine ended their qualifying run, and the pair failed to get to the starting line.

Back in Columbus in 1909, Rickenbacker followed his mentor Frayer to the Columbus Buggy Company as chief testing engineer, supervising upwards of a dozen men in his department. Frayer had been hired to design their first full-size car. The 'Torpedo Roadster' was credited as being the first car produced with a left-hand drive steering wheel. Eddie's hard work and mechanical knowledge impressed his new boss as much as they had Frayer. He chose Rickenbacker for special assignments, troubleshooting in Atlantic City and demonstrating at the 1909 Chicago automobile show. Later that year, Harvey S. Firestone, also an employee of the Buggy Company, sent this young troubleshooter to Texas to figure out why the new Frayer-designed engines were overheating. Eddie solved the problem and stayed on to head Columbus Buggy's Dallas agency. Rickenbacker was, in his own words, 'salesman, demonstrator, mechanic, the chief engineer, experimenter. I am in short, the whole ball of wax.' On one occasion he chauffeured the visiting politician William Jennings Bryan, getting his picture (and his car's) in the press. He personally made three sales as a result.

In March 1910, Firestone sent Rickenbacker to direct the Upper Midwest Agency out of Omaha. Not yet 20, Rickenbacker was in charge of six men, covering sales, distribution and maintenance of Firestone-Columbus automobiles in four states. He was earning $125 per week, more than five times the wages of a union machinist. To draw attention to his company's car, Rickenbacker entered a 25-mile race in Red Oak, Iowa.

This led to a career and an obsession. In this first race Rickenbacker failed to finish after crashing through a circuit fence. But that summer he went on to win most of the dirt track races he entered, including five out of six at Omaha's Aksarben Festival in October. The press misspelled his name Reichenbaugh, Reichenbacher and Reichenberger before settling for Rickenbacher, Richenbacher or Rickenbacker. His German-sounding name would lead to an intelligence confusion in Britain in a few years' time.

The following May, Lee Frayer invited his protégé to join him in another racing venture; the first ever Indianapolis 500. As relief driver, Rickenbacker took over from Frayer in the middle portion of the race, driving most of the miles and helping his former boss take eleventh place. The next year he drove Frayer's Red Wing Special by himself but was forced out after a hundred miles with mechanical difficulties. Nevertheless, he quit his sales job and went on the county fair circuit with the prophetically named 'Flying Squadron' team.

In October 1912 the American Automobile Association (AAA) barred Rickenbacker from the track for twelve months for flouting safety regulations; the exact nature of his misbehaviour seems unrecorded. As a result of his ban, he joined the workshop of Frederick and August Duesenberg in Des Moines, Iowa. For the next year he worked sixteen-hour days at three dollars a day developing the 'Mason' race car, named after Duesenberg's first major investor.

In July 1913, Rickenbacker was given a dispensation to compete in his hometown Columbus in a 200-mile race and somehow managed to keep his reinstatement open through the rest of the season. He won three times and finished the season in 27th place on the AAA standings with 115 points. One can speculate that it was perhaps his popularity with the crowds that encouraged the authorities to turn a blind eye to his season's return.

1914 was a make-or-break year for the Duesenberg team. Edward R. Mason had sold his interest to Frederick Maytag and now the Maytag-Mason company was on the verge of bankruptcy. If their funds ran out, Duesenberg and Rickenbacker would have to give up racing.

They were desperate as they faced the Fourth of July race at Sioux City, and hard driving gave Eddie and the team the win. That and a third-place finish by a second Duesenberg driver brought in $12,500 and the team was able to complete the season. Rickenbacker finished the year in sixth place in the AAA standings. Eddie was now established as a top racing driver and was becoming an 'all American hero'.

Rickenbacker earned the nickname 'Fast Eddie'. One sportswriter called him 'the most daring but the most cautious driver in America today'.

The top-ranked French Peugeot team lured Rickenbacker away from Duesenberg at the start of 1915. But with poor results from the start,

Eddie left the French and switched to the Maxwell team. Maxwell were an independent manufacturer producing cars between 1904 and 1925 and have long since been absorbed into what is now Fiat-Chrysler. In his autobiography Rickenbacker called the Peugeot move 'the major mistake of my racing career'. However, he still finished the season ranked fifth among all racers, with three victories to his credit.

In September 1915, Rickenbacker received financial backing from Indianapolis Speedway owner Carl Fisher and his partner Fred Allison, who made him the leader of a new Presto-Lite team. Fisher and Allison put Eddie in charge of three drivers and four mechanics in the development of four race cars they called Maxwell Specials.

With eighteen months still to go before America and Germany would declare war upon each other, Rickenbacker won the Sioux City race for the third year in a row. He also won at Tacoma and Sheepshead Bay.

In September 1916, Rickenbacker was behind Dario Resta and Johnny Aitken in a three-way race for the championship. He needed a win at the Indianapolis Harvest 100 if he was to catch the other two. He had the lead in the penultimate lap but had driven his car into the ground; Aitken passed Rickenbacker's mechanically-stricken Maxwell Special with his own car limping along on three wheels. So Eddie finished the year in third place in the standings. His final win of the season in Los Angeles would be, unknown to the racing world and to Rickenbacker himself, the last race of his career.

Signing with the Sunbeam team for the next season, Rickenbacker sailed to England to work on the development of his new car in December. Before he could disembark in Liverpool, he was detained by two plainclothes detectives from Scotland Yard. A 1914 *Los Angeles Times* article had fabricated a story of the young driver as Baron Rickenbacher, 'the disowned son of a Prussian noble'.

With Britain deep into a four-year war with Germany, Scotland Yard's Special Branch was taking no chances with a potential spy. For anyone who has read my book *Murder of Innocence*, there is a completely fact-based thread about the existence of a German spy network in Britain, with the likes of Karl Hans Lody being detained by Special Branch. Lody was held at the Tower of London before being executed as a spy.

Rickenbacker in his own words: 'I was ordered to stay on the boat and I was going to be returned without even disembarking. I had matched the description of the spy they claimed to be looking for to a 'T'. My name matched their intelligence, and so did the sailing I had undertaken. On Christmas Day I persuaded the authorities to let me spend the day on land, and I was able to get in touch with Mr Coatalen of the Sunbeam Works. He vouched for my status and he got in communication with the intelligence authorities who allowed me to proceed. I realised from the morale and status of the English officers that America would get involved in the war sooner or later.'

However, the police continued surveillance on Rickenbacker for the entire six weeks he was in England and then for another two weeks once he was back across the Atlantic and into the United States. Again, with my writing and other storytelling, there are shades of the surveillance of American Doctor Francis Tumblety following the Jack the Ripper Murders in 1888. Scotland Yard detectives pursued him to New York, another factual story recounted in the novel *Whitechapel*.

Later he decided to 'take the Hun out of his name' and officially changed it to Rickenbacker. 'From then on,' as he wrote in his autobiography, 'most Rickenbachers were practically forced to spell their name in the way I had.' After the war he decided his given name 'looked a little plain' and adopted a middle name; he settled on Vernon, after the brother of his boyhood crush, Blanche Calhoun.

Meanwhile in England, Rickenbacker worked at the Sunbeam workshop in Wolverhampton during the week, spending weekends at the Savoy Hotel in London. He frequently found himself watching Royal Flying Corps aeroplanes swoop over the Thames, having taken off from the Brooklands aerodrome at Weybridge.

In November 1916, back in Los Angeles, Rickenbacker had two chance encounters with aviators. The first was Glenn Martin, founder of the Glenn L. Martin Company and Wright-Martin Aircraft. Despite Eddie's lifelong fear of heights, Martin gave Rickenbacker his first ride into the skies.

Next he found a flyer called Major Townsend F. Dodd stranded with his plane in a field. Eddie diagnosed a magneto problem. Dodd later became General John J. Pershing's aviation officer and an important contact in Rickenbacker's career.

After the revelation of the Zimmermann Telegram, Rickenbacker shared with a *New York Times* reporter an idea he had conceived for an aero squadron composed of race car drivers and mechanics: 'War would practically put a stop to racing, and we have a training that our country would need in time of war. We are experts in judging speed and in motor knowledge.' After the

April 1917 declaration of war between Germany and the United States, Rickenbacker went to Washington to propose his idea. He was ignored. Military officials wanted college-educated men for the new aviation section, not men from the working classes. This was a prejudice that the legendary Chuck Yeager also experienced during his stellar career.

A month later, a week before he was due to race in Cincinnati, Rickenbacker was invited to be chauffeur for General John J. Pershing and given the rank of sergeant first class . By mid-June he was 'somewhere in France, driving Army officials between Paris and A.E.F. headquarters in Chaumont, and various points on the Western Front,' but he did not drive for General Pershing. He mostly drove for Major Dodd, the pilot he met in late 1916 when Dodd had broken down in his plane.

Once again, Rickenbacker made an important connection by repairing a superior's broken-down machine: he fashioned a bearing of metal in a sand mould at a country mechanic's shop for the car of Lieutenant Colonel Billy Mitchell, who is credited as being the father of the United States Air Force.

This was perhaps fateful, but it was a chance encounter with Captain James Miller on the Champs-Élysées that put Rickenbacker on the track to become a fighter pilot. Miller asked Rickenbacker to be chief engineer at the flight school and aerodrome he was establishing at Issoudun. Rickenbacker bargained with him for the chance to learn to fly at the French flight school outside Toul. He received five weeks of training and twenty-five hours in the air in September 1917. Then he went to Issoudun to start constructing the US Air Service's pursuit (fighter combat) training facility.

American aviation cadets, all college men, were just beginning to arrive for their flight training. Rickenbacker resented their cocky attitude. They scorned his rough manner and speech. This must have been difficult for a man who had grafted throughout his life to get to where he was. At 27 he was considered too old to fly, but for the next three months he stole moments from his work to continue his flight training, standing in at the back of lectures and taking aeroplanes up on his own to practice new manoeuvres. He would eventually earn the respect of the aviators, but for now he had just one ally among the cadets, Lieutenant Reed Chambers, later to become an 'air-ace' and serve with Rickenbacker in the 94th. In January 1918 Rickenbacker engineered an opportunity to get released to gunnery school, the final step on his road to becoming a pursuit pilot.

In February and March 1918 the now Lieutenant Rickenbacker and the officers of the developing 1st Pursuit Group completed their advanced training at Villeneuve-les-Vertus aerodrome. There Eddie Rickenbacker, now affectionately known as 'Rick', came under the tutelage of Major Raoul Lufbery. 'All I learned, I learned from Lufbery,' he would say. Lufbery took him on his first patrol 'over the line' before their Nieuport 28s biplanes were fitted with machine guns.

Both squadrons then relocated to Toul where Rickenbacker had begun his training with the French months earlier. The American Air Service had its own aerodrome in Gengoult nearby. They chose an insignia to paint on its planes: the 95th chose a kicking mule, the 94th chose an Uncle Sam stovepipe hat, tipped and inside a surrounding circle. One officer remarked, 'I guess our hat is in the ring now!' and the squadron became known as the 'Hat-in-the-Ring Gang'.

Rickenbacker made his first sortie with his new friend and flying comrade Reed Chambers on 13 April 1918. It almost ended in disaster when they became lost in poor visibility and Chambers had to make a forced landing. Flight Commander David Peterson called Rick a 'bloody fool for flying off in a fog'. Two weeks later, on 29 April, Rickenbacker shot down his first enemy plane. By 28 May he had claimed his fifth victory to become an ace and was awarded the French Croix de Guerre. Not all went smoothly however: several times he almost fired on friendly planes; he nearly crashed when the fabric on his Nieuport's wing tore off in a dive; his guns had a habit of jamming when he went in for the kill; and he had to mourn the death of his flying inspiration Raoul Lufbery.

On 30 May he scored his sixth victory, but it would be his last for three and a half months. He suffered a fever in late June and developed an ear infection in July which grounded him for almost all of the 'Chateau Thierry' campaign (part of the defence against the German Spring offensive of 1918). During his hospitalization in Paris Rickenbacker decided that he needed to show more self-discipline and less impetuosity if he ever got back in the air.

Rickenbacker did get back into the air in time for the St. Mihiel offensive (part of the Allied '100 Days' offensive) based out of Rembercourt aerodrome, starting from 12 September. By this time the 94th had converted from their agile but temperamental Nieuports to the more rugged, higher-powered Spad XIII. Rickenbacker liked the new machine, making his first kill on 14

September against a Fokker D-VII and another the next day. As Rickenbacker's performance was rising, the performance of the 94th Squadron as a whole had been disappointing. Major Harold Hartney, commander of the 1st Pursuit Group since late August, wanted to restore the 'Hat-in-the-Ring Gang' to its former greatness. He chose Lieutenant Rickenbacker over several other captains to become the new commander of the 94th.

Rickenbacker went straight to work turning his men 'back into a team', reminding especially the mechanics that he was one of them, stressing the crucial importance of their work. He let them know he was 'a "gimper", a bird who will stick by you through anything,' and 'would never ask anybody to do anything that he would not do himself first or do at the same time.'

The next morning Rickenbacker took a patrol over the line and shot down two enemy planes. The victories in the air above Billy in France later earned him the Congressional Medal of Honour, presented by President Hoover in 1931.

Building on the leadership skills he had first developed with the Maxwell racing team, Rickenbacker turned the 94th Squadron into a very different kind of winning team. He was determined to 'blind the eyes of the enemy' by taking out his observation balloons. The giant gas bags appeared temptingly easy to bring down, but were in fact heavily guarded and extremely dangerous to attack. He led planning sessions for raids with as many as fourteen attacking aircraft. Rickenbacker was likened by a war correspondent 'to a big-time football coach, boning up for the season ahead with conferences on methods, blackboard talks, and ideas for air battle tactics.'

Although Rickenbacker was personally credited with bringing down five balloons, this was far fewer than the air service's most prolific balloon-buster, Frank Luke of the 27th Aero Squadron, who sent fourteen German observation balloons up in flames in two weeks. Luke's productivity, however, came at the price of recklessness. An airman in Rickenbacker's squadron wrote, 'As the doctors say to the press, he is not expected to live.' Rickenbacker was hoping to get him transferred to the 94th and tame his impetuosity and make use of his talent, but he never got the chance. Frank Luke was killed five days after Rickenbacker took command of the 94th Squadron.

Rickenbacker taught his squadron the principles of engagement he had worked out while in hospital: 'Never attack unless there is at least 50-50 chance of success; always break off an engagement that seems hopeless; know the difference between cowardice and common sense.'

He also flew more patrols and more hours in the air than any other pilot in the service, a total of 300 combat hours. He brought down 15 aircraft in the final six weeks of the war, bringing his total victories to 26 and making him the USA's ace of aces for the war. It remained the American record until surpassed by Richard Bong's forty kills in the Second World War.

When Rickenbacker learned of the Armistice, he flew an aeroplane above no man's land to observe the ceasefire as it occurred at 11 am on 11 November. He later wrote: 'I was the only audience for the greatest show ever presented. On both sides of no man's land, the trenches erupted. Brown-uniformed men poured out of the American trenches, grey-green uniforms out of the German. From my observer's seat overhead, I watched them throw their helmets in the air, discard their guns, wave their hands.'

Rickenbacker was awarded the Distinguished Service Cross a record eight times. One of these was later converted into the Congressional Medal of Honour. He was also awarded the *Légion d'Honneur* and the *Croix de Guerre*. In 1919 Captain Edward Vernon Rickenbacker was discharged from the Army Air Service.

He was welcomed as a war hero on his return to America. At the Waldorf Astoria in New York six hundred friends and admirers, including Secretary of War Newton Baker and Rickenbacker's mother (shuttled in from Columbus), cheered him, toasted him, shouted and sang to him. On the streets, he described getting mobbed by souvenir seekers, tearing buttons and ribbons off his uniform. Los Angeles also gave him a hero's welcome parade in June 1919. He signed a book deal which turned into his memoir of the war, *Fighting the Flying Circus*, ghost written by Laurence la Tourette Driggs. He was contracted for a speaking tour which doubled as a promotion for Liberty Bonds.

Rickenbacker turned down several offers to endorse products, including cigarettes, as well as the opportunity to star in a feature film. After the Liberty Bond tour Rickenbacker was released from the army with the rank of major, but he chose never to use the rank, feeling that the rank of captain was the one he had earned and deserved. He was often referred to as 'Captain Eddie' or just 'the Captain' for the rest of his life.

Rickenbacker never returned to motor racing as a driver, and only dabbled in motor vehicle manufacture through the 1920s. He founded the Rickenbacker Motor Company, innovating with the development of all four wheels braking for a road car, and the tandem fly-wheel construction for engines to reduce vibration. Rivalry with Studebaker, the death of a key engineer, and a failure of Eddie's leadership, left RMC going into receivership in 1925.

But that was not the end of his career. On 1 November 1927 Rickenbacker bought the Indianapolis Motor Speedway, which he operated for a decade and a half, overseeing many improvements to the facility.

Once the motor speedway operations were under control, Rickenbacker looked for additional opportunities for entrepreneurship, including in sales for the Cadillac division of General Motors, and for various aircraft manufacturers and airlines.

After the Indy 500 of 1941 Rickenbacker closed the Speedway due to the Second World War. The race would have been a waste of valuable fuel, rubber, and other mechanical resources. After the war Rickenbacker sold the track to the businessman Anton Hulman, Jr.

In his private life, Eddie married Adelaide, the divorced wife of one of his racing rivals. They adopted two children and settled in Bronxville, New York, which remained their main residence for the rest of their lives. Through his life, he kept links with General Motors as a result of his wife's connections. But it was aviation that dominated the rest of his professional life. Eastern Airlines, that existed right up to 1991, was his key interest.

On 26 February 1941 he was a passenger on an Eastern Air Lines Douglas DC-3 that crashed just outside Atlanta, Georgia. He suffered grave injuries, being soaked in fuel, immobile, and trapped in the wreckage. In spite of his own critical wounds, Rickenbacker encouraged the other passengers, offered what consolation he could to those around him who were injured or dying, and guided the survivors who were still mobile to find help. The survivors were rescued after spending the night at the crash site. Rickenbacker barely survived. The press announced his death while he was still alive; his injuries were so devastating that medical staff had dismissed him as dead or dying, both at the scene and at the hospital. His injuries included a compressed fractured skull, a shattered left elbow with a crushed nerve, a paralyzed left hand, several broken ribs, a crushed hip socket, his pelvis broken in two places, a severed nerve in his left hip, and a broken left knee. His left eyeball was also blown out of its socket. But he recovered.

Eastern Airlines was one of many carriers who sent supplies to the UK in the war. In 1942, with a letter of authorization from Henry L. Stimson, US Secretary of War, Rickenbacker visited England on an official war mission.

He worked with both the RAF and the USAAF on bombing strategy, including work with Air Chief Marshal Sir Arthur Harris.

In October 1942, having been sent to look at military operations in the Pacific, a battered B-17 he was travelling in was forced to ditch in a remote area of the central Pacific Ocean. For twenty-four days Rickenbacker and seven others were adrift in several life rafts tied together. Their food ran out after the first three days, and at one point Rickenbacker managed to grab a seagull that landed on his head, kill it and feed the group with it. The group eventually split up. Rickenbacker was reported dead, but his wife insisted the US forces did not abandon the search. Rickenbacker and all the others but one, who had died, were found alive in their separate groups.

In 1943 Rickenbacker completed a mission to Russia to advise on the use of American-supplied aircraft. The mission eventually took on wider parameters, observing the Soviet war effort and reporting back to the West on the social and economic fabric of Soviet society. He met with Winston Churchill as a result.

'The Captain' Eddie Rickenbacker suffered a stroke while in Switzerland seeking special medical treatment for his wife, and subsequently contracted pneumonia. He died on 23 July 1973 in Zürich. A memorial service was held at the Key Biscayne Presbyterian Church with the eulogy given by another American war hero, Lieutenant General Jimmy Doolittle. His body was interred in Columbus, Ohio, at the Green Lawn Cemetery. At the time of his death, he was the last living Medal of Honour recipient of the First World War Air Service, US Army.

In 1977, at the age of 92, Adelaide Rickenbacker was blind, suffering from failing health, and still grieving from the loss of her husband. She committed suicide by gunshot at their second home on Key Biscayne, Florida.

Chapter 9

Enzo Ferrari (1898-1988)

3rd Italian Mountain Artillery in the First World War

Motor racing icon

Enzo Anselmo Ferrari was said to have been born on 18 February 1898 in Modena and that his birth was recorded on 20 February because a heavy snowstorm prevented his father from reporting the birth at the local registry office. His birth certificate states he was born on 20 February 1898.

He was the younger of two children born to Alfredo Ferrari and Adalgisa Bisbini. He was brother to Alfredo Junior, 'Alfredino', known as Dino. Alfredo Senior was the son of a grocer from Carpi and started a workshop fabricating metal parts at the family home. Enzo grew up with little formal education.

Modena has historically been a centre for craftmanship in metalwork, beginning with cartwheels and axles for carts, then evolving into parts for motor vehicles. A dozen of these men became a natural labour force for Alfredo Senior's metal-working business. Enzo and his brother shared a bedroom over the workshop and woke each day to the sound of striking hammers in the rooms below them. Enzo recalled his father as fastidious in business, but also a cultured man who loved music. Alfredo kept his records meticulously with copies of correspondence made in violet ink from duplicating paper. Enzo wrote with violet ink in his fountain pen for the rest of his life. In 1903 Alfredo Senior acquired a motor car, one of only twenty-seven in Modena, a French De Dion Bouton.

At the age of 10 Enzo witnessed Felice Nazzaro's win at the 1908 Circuito di Bologna. He was entranced by the victory of the 27-year-old blue-eyed boy from Turin. The Fiat he drove at an average speed of 74 mph over the 50-kilometre course was painted red, the national colour designated in new regulations. The Germans were designated white, France blue and Britain green.

In 1913 he was determined to become a racing driver, but he received a beating over poor school reports from his father, who insisted he must become an engineer.

He achieved some note the following year when as a 16-year-old he had his reports of football matches published in *La Gazzetta dello Sport*.

Italy would not enter the Great War on the side of the Allies (Entente Powers) until May 1915, fighting against the Austro-Hungarian Empire on the Alpine front, where they fought in perilous and harsh conditions in a network of trenches carved into high mountain ranges.

The youth of Italy, especially in the north, had grown up with an endemic hatred of the Austro-Hungarians, so the army had no problem recruiting.

Enzo's older brother Dino used the family's Diatto Torpedo car as an ambulance, transporting wounded from the Alpine trenches to hospitals in the Po Valley. When he was 19, Dino enlisted in the Italian Air Force. He became a member of the ground crew for squadron 912A, the insignia for which was a set of aviator's wings and a prancing horse. This symbol was carried on the fuselage of the plane of the squadron's most famous ace, Francesco Baracca, who achieved thirty-four kills before his Spad S-13 biplane crashed on the front line killing him in 1918.

1916 was the first of two challenging years for Enzo. Italy was suffering a pneumonia outbreak and in February Alfredo Senior died and the metal fabrication business that he had established in Modena collapsed. He had died within days of becoming sick. Enzo had neither the appetite nor it seems the ability to make the Ferrari business work. He drifted through a series of menial jobs, apprenticing for a time with the Modena fire department, then taking instruction in a lathe operator's school and finding a position as a trainee in a factory manufacturing artillery shells. He drifted through his later teenage years waiting to be old enough to be called to military service.

Then 'Alfredino', the older brother he idolised, fell sick in a less-than-sanitary military camp. He was transported to a sanatorium in Sortenna di Sondrio where he died of either influenza, typhoid or perhaps some other disease.

In 1917, aged 19, Enzo was finally drafted into the Italian army, who at the time were mired in trench warfare with the Austro-Hungarians from the Isonzo River north-east of Venice to the peaks of the Dolomites and the Alto Trentino in the west. Enzo was assigned to the Third Mountain Artillery who were entrenched in a stalemate position against their adversaries in the Val Serianna mountains north of Bergamo.

Enzo claimed a background in motor mechanics, thinking he would be assigned to maintenance duties servicing the huge Breda artillery pieces. However, a Piedmontese second lieutenant assigned him to farrier duties, shoeing the mules used as beasts of burden by the artillery.

Because of Enzo's humble background, he was given shabby billets and menial duties. After three months he almost went the way of his father and brother, being hospitalised with pleurisy. He underwent surgery in Brescia, twice, to remove fluid from his lungs. He was then sent to a hospital for the incurably ill in Bologna where it was the policy to leave those with breathing complaints out in cold fresh air. Enzo recalled that he could hear workmen hammering coffin lids shut as he lay shivering and pondering his future at night. He was eventually, with minimal treatment and support, discharged from the hospital.

He saw a short return to service as the driver of a Fiat for a logistics officer called Pacchiani, and on the morning of 11 November 1918 he awoke from a night sleeping on a bag of onions to discover that the Armistice had been announced. Enzo recalled, 'I saw a group of workers changing the blueish light bulb of curfew lighting on a streetlamp for a white one. That was how I knew the war was over.'

He returned to Modena with no idea of what to do next. He said, 'I was back where I started, with no money, no experience, and a limited education, but with a passion to get somewhere.' Although equipped with a letter of reference, he was turned down for a job with Fiat in Turin. He found himself sitting on a bench on the banks of the River Po in tears: 'My father and my brother were no more. I was overcome by loneliness and despair.' He once heard his mother say, 'I lost the wrong son.' She was the only woman Ferrari was afraid of in his life.

Enzo eventually got a job as test driver for CMN (Costruzioni Meccaniche Nazionali), a car manufacturer in Milan. CMN rebuilt used truck bodies into small passenger cars. He was later promoted to their racing division and made his competitive debut in the 1919 Parma-Poggio di Berceto hill climb, in which he finished fourth in the 3.0 litre category at the wheel of a 2.3 litre 4-cylinder CMN 15/20. On 23 November 1919 he took part in the Targa Florio but had to retire after his fuel tank developed a leak. Due to the large numbers of retirements, he finished ninth.

In 1920, Enzo joined the racing department of Alfa Romeo as a driver. Alfa Romeo developed as a result of a collaboration between the original main brand 'Anonima Lombarda Fabbrica Automobili' and entrepreneur Nicola Romeo.

In 1921 in Turin Enzo met his future wife Laura Domenica Garello. He described her as 'pretty, blonde and graceful'. They married in 1923.

Ferrari won his first Grand Prix with Alfa Romeo in 1923 in Ravenna on the Savio circuit, but he was deeply affected by the death of Ugo Sivocci that season, a friend he made in a Milanese café who had got him his job at CMN. At Monza, with Alfa facing opposition from Fiat, Sunbeam and Bugatti, their team comprised Antonio Ascari, Giuseppe Campari and Sivocci. Enzo was only driving in practice sessions. Two laps into the race Sivocci's car left the track at high spend on a left-hand bend. Enzo rushed to the scene and recalled, 'I was one of the first to reach him, I gathered him into my arms and tried to give him first aid, but there was sadly nothing anyone could do for him.' The rest of the team was withdrawn from the race, and the car's number, 17, was never used again on Italian cars. Sivocci was to be the first of many drivers Enzo would mourn.

1924 was Enzo's best season, with three wins in five races, including Ravenna, Polesine and the Coppa Acerbo in Pescara, beating future stars Tazio Nuvolari and Guiseppe Campari.

At the French Grand Prix held at Lyons on 3 August Enzo felt so shattered and unwell after the practice session that he withdrew from the race. It was a strange decision off the back of three consecutive wins in ten weeks, but he said, 'My indisposition was so grave as to cut down on and compel me to practically give up driving.' He had been run-down all year, and one wonders if it was an onset of depression, a malady from which he would later suffer.

He returned home to gather his thoughts and energy and six weeks later was back with Alfa Romeo at Monza where he helped his team secure victory over Fiat. Sir Henry Segrave would set the fastest lap at Lyons, with Campari winning the race for Alfa Romeo, and Frenchman Robert Benoist coming third.

During his step away from racing, Enzo further established himself within the commerce of the motor trade, becoming the Alfa Romeo dealer for the Emilia-Romagna region. During a state tour of the region by Mussolini, Enzo drove the 'pilot' car.

The Alfa Romeo team was upbeat about the 1925 season, but the heart was torn out of them in July when Antonio Ascari died at the French Grand Prix. Enzo and Antonio were close; Antonio had admired Enzo's ability to combine business and sport, and his modesty in asking for assistance. After the death of Ascari, Ferrari admitted that he raced half-heartedly. At the end of the 1925 season, although they won the world championship, Alfa Romeo withdrew from racing.

In 1927 Enzo met Peppino Verdelli who would go on to be his chauffeur and assistant for the next forty years.

The first Mille Miglia was run in 1927 with Enzo managing a team of three privately entered Alfas, none of which completed the race. Enzo would have some involvement in the Mille Miglia for the next thirty years.

Enzo returned to racing in 1928, winning at Circuito di Alessandria and Modena.

The 1929 season saw the birth of his own racing team, the Societa Anonima Scuderia Ferrari, with investment from Alfa Romeo, Pirelli and Shell. The Scuderia Ferrari's first appearance was in the Mille Miglia of 1930. At the end of the year Scuderia Ferrari statistics read well: 50 entries in 72 events, 8 wins and several podium finishes. Enzo's final race record consisted of 41 Grand Prix with 11 wins.

In 1931, at the age of 33, Enzo made his last appearance as a racing driver. He now decided to focus on the management and development of the factory, with its new headquarters in Modena. He was building up a team of superstar drivers, including Campari and Nuvolari.

Dino, christened Alfredo after his grandfather and dead uncle, was born in January 1932. Later he would be diagnosed with Duchenne's muscular dystrophy, a rare condition that attacks the muscle cells. He would live to the age of 24, but the affliction would cause a lifelong rift between Enzo and Laura.

Enzo, however, had begun a liaison with a lady named Lina Lardi three years earlier, who lived in a hilltop village near Modena. With her Enzo would father another child, Piero, who he would not recognise publicly as his son and heir until after Laura's death.

In 1932 Scuderia Ferrari introduced the prancing horse emblem for their cars which Francesco Baracca had sported on his aeroplane in 1918. Enzo said, 'I was introduced to Baracca's father Count Enrico Baracca in Modena in 1923 and went on to meet his wife. Countess Paolina told me to put the prancing horse of her son's plane on my cars as it will bring you luck. I kept the horse black but added the yellow background as it is the colour of Modena.'

At the end of 1932 Alfa Romeo was effectively nationalised by Mussolini to build military vehicles for his imperial pursuits. At the start of 1933 Alfa declared a suspension in its production of competition cars, so Enzo began to look to other manufacturers to supply Ferrari.

Another personal tragedy befell Enzo in September; his friend and team driver Giuseppe Campari was killed at Monza.

The Ferrari team achieved a notable victory in 1935 when Nuvolari beat Caracciola and Rosemeyer on the Nürburgring. Of Nuvolari, Enzo said in later years, 'There has been only one great racing driver. There is a perfect balance between man and machine, 50% man and 50% machine. With Nuvolari this relationship was overwhelmed, he contributed 75% to the total.' For a man who believed in the superiority of his product this was quite an admission. Nuvolari won the Italian championship that year.

In 1937 Alfa Romeo decided to regain full control of their racing division and retained Enzo Ferrari as their sporting director. Alfa had been encouraged to return to racing by Mussolini as he wanted to see Italian cars beat German cars. Alfa Romeo bought an 80% stake in the Societa Anonima Scuderia Ferrari.

The team continued to have success in the Mille Miglia, but that was about all they succeeded in. Scuderia Ferrari ceased to exist from January 1938 with Alfa Romeo buying up the shares and moving the operation to Milan.

With his team dissolved, Ferrari moved to Alfa's racing team, named 'Alfa Corse'. Enzo's new contract stated that he could not manufacture cars under his own name for four years should he leave the company. He was paid well, but effectively became an employee of the company.

After one disagreement too many within the racing division, Alfa's chairman Ugo Gobbato decided to dismiss Enzo in the summer of 1939. Enzo returned to Modena thinking, 'The time had come to see how far I could get by my own efforts.'

Enzo founded 'Auto-Avio Costruzioni', whose primary purpose was the manufacture of aircraft parts. Soon he had a workforce of over forty. He knew how to produce cars if he wished, but he was not allowed to use the name Ferrari. There was no Mille Miglia in 1939; it had been banned after an accident in which ten people were killed. But it was brought back in 1940, on a closed course. Enzo was approached by two clients to produce cars for them, one of them Antonio Ascari's son Alberto.

In 1940, at 42 Enzo was too old for war service. He had been a member of the fascist party since 1934, but very much out of convenience rather than conviction.

By 1942 the Ferrari factory was producing aircraft engines. In December it moved from Modena, a likely bombing target, to Maranello about ten miles to the south. In July 1943, by which time the Allies had landed in Sicily and *Il Duce* had been deposed, Enzo was employing 100 people and making good profits. In January 1944 the Allies landed at Anzio, and in November the factory was hit by a bombing raid. The damage was still being repaired in April 1945.

Also in April 1945, the man who had sacked Ferrari from Alfa Romeo, Ugo Gobbato, who was a loyal Fascist Party member, was killed by an anonymous assassin.

Two weeks after VE Day, Enzo's mistress Lina Lardi gave birth to Piero.

In 1946 Ferrari had a brief collaboration with Maserati, but it was 1947 before he was back producing cars, unveiling a prototype on 12 March. Now he was allowed to produce under his own name again, and he founded Ferrari S.p.A.

Enzo's first post-war car entered competition in 1947, the V-12 135S at Piacenza. As had been his habit since the 1930s, and would become a life-long preference, he did not attend the races, he just waited for the telephone to ring at home. One car withdrew after practice, the other showed promise but did not complete the race.

In July 1947 Nuvolari returned to the team. He was now 54 and suffering from emphysema after all the petrochemical fumes he had inhaled. But he won races for Ferrari straight away.

In October 1947 Raymond Sommer won the Turin Grand Prix. This was the first ever Grand Prix won by Ferrari as an independent constructor. Enzo was ecstatic. He returned to the banks of the Po where he had wept for his father and brother: 'I went and sat on that very same bench, but any tears I shed were of a very different kind.'

By the end of 1947 Ferrari were producing cars for customers, starting with the 166 Spider Corsa.

In 1948 Ferrari won the Targa Florio and the Mille Miglia. The company had been constructing cars for barely a year. They came third in the Grand Prix in Turin in 1948, again with Raymond Sommer at the wheel, and later in the year Giuseppe Farina won for them the Circuito del Garda.

1930 Le Mans winners
Glen Kidston (L), Woolf
Barnato (R) with (L) Dick
Watney and (R) Frank
Clement, the crew of the
second place Bentley.

Sir Henry De Hare Segrave.

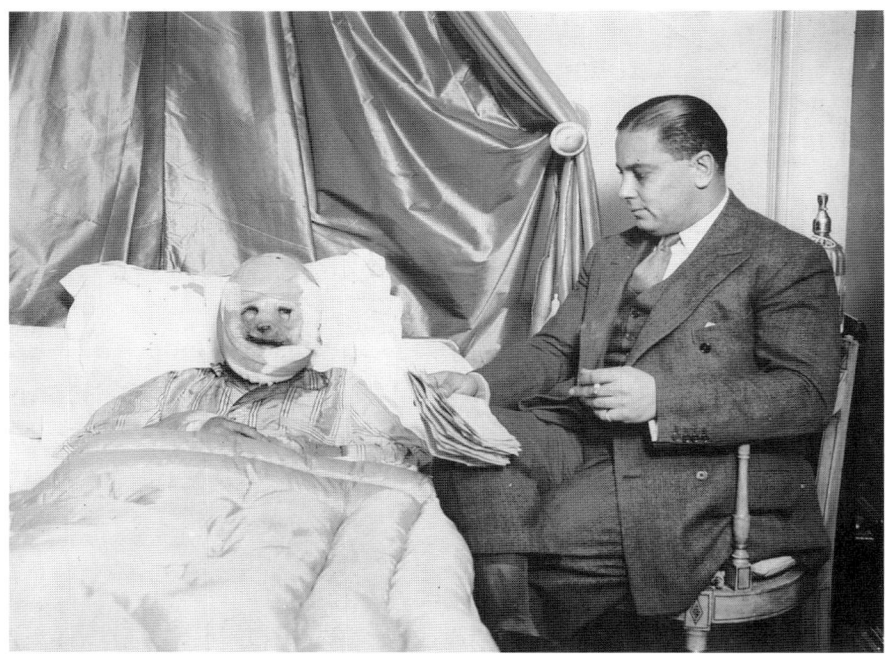

Kidston in hospital following his air crash with Barnato seated.

Woolf Barnato.

The Sporting Minis

Above: Raymond Baxter at the 'Montes' (Monte Carlo rally).

Right: Flight Lieutenant Raymond Baxter.

Below: The Bentley Boys at Mount Street Gardens 1929, Mayfair. L-R Frank Clement, Sammy Davis, Dudley Benjafield, Bernard Rubin, Woolf Barnato & Tim Birkin.

Sir Tim Birkin.

2nd Lieut.
Henry Ralph Stanley Birkin.
(2nd Bn. Sherwood Foresters)
5871   2 Aug, 1916

Second Lt Tim Birkin.

Captain Murray Walker.

Above left: Captain Robert Benoist.

Above right: David Purley in the driving seat.

Right: The Duke of Kent with Barnato and Davis.

Above: Gwenda Hawkes.

Left: Captain Eddie Rickenbacker.

Gwenda Hawkes with rival Kaye Petre.

Above left: Enzo Ferrari.

Above right: Glen Kidston in his racing overalls.

Ken Miles, 'the USA West Coast's 'Stirling Moss'.

John Duff, fencing coach and stunt man.

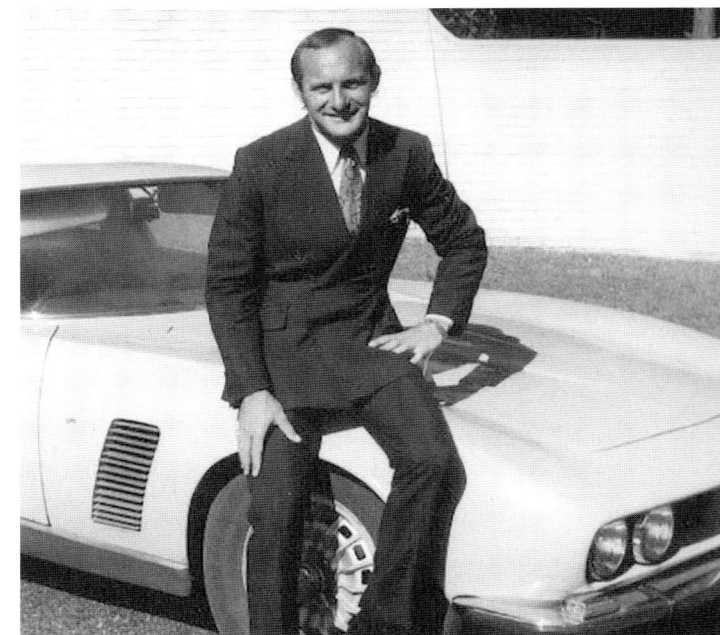

Mike Hailwood with his Iso Grifo car.

Hailwood during his motorcycling comeback.

Second Lt Carroll Shelby.

Above: Muriel racing in 1908.

Left: Muriel Thompson MM.

Right: Muriel Thompson's grave at the Brompton Cemetery, London.

Below: Murray Walker with his father Graham in Europe.

Above: Purley (R) on exercise possibly in Aden.

Right: Second Lt Purley in the field possibly in Aden.

Eddie Rickenbacker in a Maxwell in his racing days.

Above left: Bernard Rubin.

Above middle: Staff Sergeant Ken Miles.

Above right: Sammy Davis in his racing attire.

Carroll Shelby and Ken Miles at the height of the partnership.

Robert Benoist in his racing days.

Chief Petty Officer SCH Sammy
Davis of the RNAS, WW1.

Above: Major Sammy
Davis of the REME,
WW2.

Left: Lt Commander
Glen Kidston.

Right: Author with HMQ.

Below: Major Henry Segrave with his dog 'Laddie' and his 60bhp 'Apperson' car.

Left: The David Purley
GM memorial at
Bognor Regis.

Below: Niall McCarthy's
(#eastcorkpainter)
painting of David
Purley attempting to
save Roger Williamson.
Kindly licensed for use
in this publication by
Niall.

The text on the memorial:

David
Charles
Purley
GM

1945

1985

George
Medal

Gone now your eager smile
High held head and soldiers stride
Etched were skies by your elegant style
And the earth enriched by your pride

Aged 17, Dino began to be seen around the Ferrari works, learning the ways of automobile engineering at both the factory and also at the technical college at Modena. He was a handsome, dark haired boy watching testing from the shadows but struggling with his illness.

Meanwhile, the 166 models appeared at the Turin motor show in late 1948, creating a sensation with the elements of luxury they possessed as well as their performance. A win with a 166MM at the Mille Miglia in 1949 gave Enzo his second 'brand' win in the race. But this was nothing in comparison to his next success.

The first victory bringing truly international recognition for the Ferrari marque came in the 1949 24 Hours of Le Mans, the first one since the war, with a Ferrari 166MM driven by Luigi Chinetti and Baron Selsdon of Scotland, Peter Mitchell-Thomson. Many of the Ferrari brand's greatest victories came at Le Mans – nine of them, including six in a row in 1960-65.

To finance their racing endeavours, Ferrari had to be selling sports cars for the road, ideally internationally. Chinetti was instrumental in establishing Ferrari sales in the USA.

In 1950 Ferrari enrolled in the newly-founded Drivers' World Championship – and Ferrari remains today the only team to have competed every year in what is now referred to as Formula One.

In 1949 Stirling Moss had caught the eye of Ferrari as a considerable talent. He had given chase to the Italians in several inferior cars, so Enzo let it be known that he was interested in offering him a seat. Moss drove to Modena to see him. They seemed to get on well, conversing in French, and an agreement was made that Moss would drive a Ferrari at Bari in September 1951. Moss made the considerable journey to Bari with his father to find the seat had been promised to another driver. He was furious, and through the rest of his career Moss would take great delight in beating the cars from Maranello whenever he had the chance.

In August 1953 Enzo's favourite driver died at home in the arms of his wife. Tazio Nuvolari's lungs finally gave out.

Late in 1954 it was rumoured that due to Dino's deteriorating health Enzo was considering withdrawing from Formula One. However, he remained in the championship but competed only in the major calendar events. This was the year of Fangio's great successes with Mercedes and Maserati.

Ferrari's decision to continue racing in the Mille Miglia brought the company new victories and increased public recognition, but trouble was soon to come. The increasing speeds, poor roads and non-existent crowd protection eventually spelled disaster for both the race and Ferrari. During the 1957 Mille Miglia near the town of Guidizzolo a 4.0 litre Ferrari 335S being driven by Alfonso de Portago was traveling at 250 km/h when it blew a tyre and crashed into the roadside crowd. It killed de Portago, his co-driver and nine spectators, five of whom were children. Enzo Ferrari and Englebert the Belgian tyre manufacturer were charged with manslaughter, but after a lengthy criminal prosecution the case was finally dismissed.

In 1961 Ferrari supported Bologna-based publisher Luciano Conti's decision to start a new publication called *Autosprint*. Ferrari himself regularly contributed to the magazine, driven partly by the desire for accurate copy after the Mille Miglia tragedy.

Fangio signed with Ferrari for the 1956 season following Mercedes' withdrawal from racing after the Le Mans tragedy of 1955 when Pierre Levagh's Mercedes cartwheeled into the crowd having struck the rear of Mike Hawthorn's car. Levagh (racing as Bouillin) was killed along with eighty-three spectators.

Fangio won the 1956 season, but on 30 June that year Dino died at home in Modena. Enzo wrote in a notebook: 'The game is lost'. The mid-engine V6 which Dino had begun was, of course, named after him.

Enzo Ferrari possessed a strong personality and controversial management style that became notorious. He was not known as Il Commendatore without good reason.

In 1961 Ferrari suffered a defection of managers. Sales manager Girolamo Gardini, manager Romolo Tavoni, chief engineer Carlo Chiti, sports car development chief Giotto Bizzarini, and others left to form rival car manufacturer and racing team 'Automobili Turismo e Sport'.

This came at a difficult time for Enzo. The investigation of the fatal Mille Miglia accident had only concluded a year before, Ferrari driver Count Wolfgang von Trips had been killed in 1961, and Enzo still hadn't recovered from the death of his son. Enzo had effectively withdrawn from the day to day activities of running both his racing team and his sports car companies, but someone else had taken over. That person was the headstrong and difficult Laura. She already had a reputation for prowling the factory when she had a minor role in the Ferrari operation, but now she was effectively its CEO and was uncompromising. The workforce complained to her, but she berated them, screaming at them and making them fear for their jobs.

Gardini went to see the Commendatore, but Enzo fired him, making him leave by the back door. The other managers then met with Enzo. During a 45-minute confrontation he said nothing, but after the meeting was over Enzo's secretary handed them all an envelope each with a month's pay and they were told never to come back.

In 1998, Romolo Tavoni said in an interview that he and the other managers were ousted following a disagreement with Ferrari over the role of his wife in the company. He said, 'Our mistake was to go to a lawyer and write him a letter, instead of openly discussing the issue with him. We knew that his wife wasn't well. We should have been able to deal with it in a different way. When he called the meeting to fire us, he had already nominated our successors.'

Now Enzo was forced to ponder the solvency of the company. There were several lawsuits following fatal accidents, rivals Shelby and Jaguar were in the ascendant, his chief engineer for the 250 GTO (Bizzarini) had gone, and Lotus won the F1 constructors' championship.

At the urging of engineer Carlo Chiti the company had been developing a new 250-based model. Even if the car could be finished it was unclear whether it could be raced successfully. But engineer Mauro Forghieri had remained on the staff. The mid-engine Dino V6 laid the foundation for the dominant 250P.

In 1963 Enzo rejected a takeover bid by Ford. After that Henry Ford II was determined to beat Ferrari at all costs and employed former racing driver Carroll Shelby to help. Shelby had turned down driving for Ferrari and had beaten them at Le Mans in 1959 driving an Aston Martin. Ford and Ferrari split the decade between them at Le Mans.

By the end of the 1960s, increasing financial difficulties forced Ferrari to look for a business partner. In 1969 he sold 50% of his company to Fiat, but he retained 100% control of the racing activities. Fiat would pay for use of his Maranello and Modena production plants. In 1988 after Enzo's death Fiat's holding rose to 90%.

In 1971 Enzo Ferrari stepped down as managing director of the road car division, and in 1974 he appointed Luca Cordero di Montezemolo as Sporting Director/Formula One team manager. Montezemolo would eventually assume the presidency of Ferrari in 1992.

Clay Regazzoni was runner up in the Formula One championship of 1974, and Niki Lauda won it for Ferrari in 1975 and 1977. In 1977 Ferrari was criticized in the press for replacing Lauda with newcomer Gilles Villeneuve.

Ferrari claimed that Villeneuve's aggressive driving style reminded him of his greatest driver Nuvolari.

After Jody Scheckter won the Formula One world title in 1979, the team experienced a disastrous 1980. In 1981 Ferrari attempted to revive his team's fortunes by switching to turbo engines. In 1982 the second turbo-powered Ferrari (the 126C2) showed great promise. However, in May Gilles Villeneuve was killed in an accident during the last session of free practice for the Belgian Grand Prix in Zolder. In August, at Hockenheim, teammate Didier Pironi had his career cut short in a violent end-over-end flip on the misty back straight after hitting the Renault driven by Alain Prost. Pironi was leading the driver's championship at the time; he would lose the lead as he was forced to sit out the remaining races. The Scuderia went on to win the Constructors' Championship at the end of the season and again in 1983, but the team would not see championship glory again before Ferrari's death in 1988. The final race win in Enzo's lifetime was when Gerhard Berger and Michele Alboreto scored a 1-2 finish in the last round of the 1987 season in Australia. Not that the Commendatore would have travelled to see it.

Ferrari was known to pit drivers against each other in the hope of improving their performance. 'He thought that psychological pressure would produce better results for the drivers,' said Tony Brooks. He had driven for Ferrari in 1959. 'He would expect a driver to go beyond reasonable limits. You can drive to the maximum of your ability, but once you start psyching yourself up to do things that you don't feel are within your ability it gets stupid. There was enough danger at that time without going over the limit.' It was something Fangio disliked when he drove for Ferrari.

During the late 50s and into the 60s seven drivers were killed driving Ferrari racing cars: Alberto Ascari, Eugenio Castellotti, Alfonso de Portago, Luigi Musso, Peter Collins, Wolfgang von Trips and Lorenzo Bandini. Although such a high death toll was not unusual in motor racing in those days, the Vatican newspaper *L'Osservatore Romano* described Ferrari as being like the god Saturn, who consumed his own sons. In Ferrari's defence Stirling Moss commented, 'I can't think of a single occasion where a Ferrari driver's life was taken because of mechanical failure.'

In public Ferrari was careful to acknowledge the drivers who risked their life for his team. However his long-time friend and company accountant, Carlo Benzi, admitted that privately Ferrari would say that 'the car was the reason for any success,' perhaps with the exception of Nuvolari.

Following the deaths of Campari in 1933 and Ascari in 1955, he chose not to get close to his drivers for fear of emotionally hurting himself. Later in life he relented this position however, and Regazzoni and Villeneuve became close friends.

Ferrari rarely granted interviews, indeed he seldom left Modena and Maranello. He did usually go to Monza and Imola, but he never went to a Grand Prix outside Italy after the 1950s. He never flew in an aeroplane and never set foot in a lift.

As divorce was illegal in Italy until 1975, Piero could only be recognized as Enzo's son after Laura's death in 1978. Piero is currently the vice chairman of the Ferrari company.

Enzo Ferrari died on 14 August 1988 in Maranello at the age of 90. In 2002 the first car to be named after him was the Ferrari Enzo.

The Italian Grand Prix was held a few weeks after Ferrari's death, and the result was a 1-2 finish for Ferrari, Gerhard Berger leading home Italian teammate Michele Alboreto.

After Ferrari's death the Scuderia Ferrari team has continued to achieve huge success. It won the Formula One drivers' championship for five consecutive seasons from 2000 to 2004 with Michael Schumacher and then in 2007 with Kimi Räikkönen; and it won the constructors' championship from 1999 to 2004 and then in 2007 and 2008.

Chapter 10

Muriel Thompson (1875-1939)

First Aid Nursing Yeomanry in the First World War

Brooklands Racer and Military Medal Recipient

The world has been blessed with many trail blazers in all disciplines and professions, but Scotland produced a young woman who put the capital letters on the words 'Trail Blazer': Muriel Annie Thompson, born at 17 Albyn Place, Aberdeen, on 10 June 1875, the fifth of eight children. She went on to become a racing driver, a military ambulance driver, a suffragist, and won the Military Medal. Her parents were shipowner and marine architect Cornelius Thompson and Agnes Marion Williamson, his second wife. Her grandfather George Thompson had been Lord Provost of the city and an MP. It was him who had founded the George Thompson Shipping Company, known later as the Aberdeen White Star line. After the death of her father Muriel lived with her mother in London at 48 Queen's Gate, Kensington.

Muriel and her two full brothers, Walter and Oscar, were keen drivers. She won a 'blindfolded dash' in a motor gymkhana at a young age.

On 4 July 1908 Muriel won the Ladies' Bracelet Handicap, the very first race held at Brooklands for women drivers. She drove her brother Oscar's racing Austin nicknamed 'Pobble' at an average speed of 50 mph.

The women had their long skirts tied around their ankles, both to stop them snagging on their cars and to avoid 'flashing their knees'. Each wore colourful scarves and adopted 'interesting and varying driving styles'. Some sat bolt upright, others almost lay flat; Muriel in 'Pobble' hunched herself over the steering wheel like a jockey. She shunned goggles as they were 'far too hideous'. After the race Muriel was greeted with shouts of 'Women deserve the vote now!' She agreed with the sentiment and was subsequently hired as a chauffeur for the Women's Social and Political Union, driving Emmeline Pankhurst on her national tour. Their car was a green Austin with white wheels and purple stripes, the colours of the suffragette movement.

A month later she raced against Christabel Ellis and won, again at Brooklands, in the last women's race Brooklands allowed until 1928. It also appears to have been Muriel's last involvement in the world of motor racing.

At the outbreak of the First World War, Oscar joined a volunteer ambulance convoy formed to assist the French, taking 'Pobble', the Austin now splendidly converted into an ambulance. Muriel would have joined too, but women were not welcome to join this venture, so she turned to the First Aid Nursing Yeomanry Corps (FANY), an organisation founded in 1907 by Captain Edward Baker:

During my period of service with Lord Kitchener in the Soudan Campaign, where I had the misfortune to be wounded, it occurred to me that there was a missing link somewhere in the Ambulance Department which, in spite of the changes in warfare, had not altered very materially since the days of Crimea when Florence Nightingale and her courageous band of helpers went out to succour and save the wounded.

On my return from active service I thought out a plan which I anticipated would meet the want, but it was not until September 1907 that I was able to establish a troop of young women to see how my ideas on the subject would work. My idea was that each member of this Corps would receive, in addition to a thorough training in First Aid, a drilling in cavalry movements, signalling and camp work, so that nurses could ride onto the battlefield to attend to the wounded who might otherwise have been left to a slow death.

Baker soon after disappeared from the scene and the corps came under the control of two determined women, Lilian Franklin and Grace Ashley-Smith. They acquired a horse-drawn ambulance, replaced the elaborate uniform with more practical khaki, and introduced astride riding (with divided skirts to assist). Although often subjected to scorn and hostility from the general public, they gained the support of the Brigade of Guards, the Army Medical Corps (RAMC) and the Surrey Yeomanry, all of whom helped to train them at their annual camp.

The first contingent of FANYs was at Fenchurch Street station waiting for the boat-train when the news of the fall of Antwerp came through. The first small troop of six FANYs left for France on 27 October 1914: three nurses, two orderlies and Grace Ashley-Smith's brother, Bill. In Calais they found hundreds of wounded men on stretchers or lying on straw on the quayside awaiting boats to England. On 29 October they took over a dirty and decaying convent school opposite the Église Notre Dame. This was to be Lamarck hospital. The wounded were being brought in before the FANYs had time to unpack.

The FANYs also drove ambulances for the Belgian and French armies on the Western Front. Their greatest appeal turned out to be their motoring skills, rare in women at that time. Vehicles were scarce in Calais in those early months and the one FANY ambulance was in much demand.

Muriel Thompson joined the FANY in early 1915 and set off for France on 8 February. On arrival she drove from Calais to the hospital at Lamarck. She kept a diary throughout her war service. These are early entries:

Feb 23rd

Left Calais with White and Waite. We were to go beyond Pervyse to take bundles of shirts, socks, etc, the Belgians being very badly in need of supplies. We started early on a glorious morning and motored through a flat, ugly country towards Gravelines, a pretty, unfortified town which reminded me of Banbury. Then on to Dunkirk, a strongly fortified place, and so into Belgium. We stopped at Furnes, a very quaint little place with a lovely old church. It is like a city of the dead, every house was shuttered and only a few soldiers were to be seen walking about. The beautiful old square is damaged in places but this was nothing to what Pervyse is like. It is simply in ruins: church, houses, shops, all destroyed. The road had got very bad after Furnes, narrow pave in the middle and deep mud ruts on each side, awful if a back wheel slipped off. A long way after Pervyse, we reached the second line trenches. We went one at a time and left about one hundred yards between us so as not to draw the German fire. As I was walking along I heard the whizz of the shrapnel for the first time. There is no mistaking it, first a bang, then a curious whistling, swishing sound. Then another bang, then a white smoke cloud bursting and lingering some time. All the time the larks were singing and the shrapnel was going on. We ploughed along in the most awful mud I have ever seen. Every now and then we would stop and a head would appear out of a hole and a man would dive out on all fours. 'How many are you?' And then we would give as many packets of cigarettes as there were men and hand out shirts, socks, etc, and newspapers. A number of men had been wounded in the bombardment. We helped them back as fast as we could to a little [...] but where there were stretchers and then to the car.

March 30th

Had the shock of my life. Was very tired and had headache so stayed in bed when woken by Chris Nicholson banging on the door and saying, 'Get up at once, you've got the Leopold II, and you must go to La Panne to get it.' I did not know what she was talking about. At first I thought she was talking about the hospital ship and that I must get up and take some men there. I dressed in a hurry, rushed to the hospital and found an order had come for us to present ourselves at the Royal Villa at La Panne to be decorated by King Albert.

On 30 March Muriel was awarded the 'Chevalier of the Order of Leopold II' by King Albert for her bravery in evacuating wounded Belgian soldiers under fire near Dixmunde.

Over the years the FANYs learned to drive a wide variety of vehicles. Among many others there was a Ford ambulance named 'Flossie', and Muriel's own was a Cadillac named 'Kangaroo'. She adopted a pragmatic approach to maintenance:

Flossie's carburettor flooded after lunch. I hit it with a spanner and it revived. Parcels arrived from England – joy! A cake from Buzzard, also a lovely oil pump and pliers, just what I wanted.

On 16 March 1915 there was a Zeppelin raid on Calais. Every window in the hospital was smashed and splintered over the patients' beds. Beryl Hutchinson, another FANY, described the scene:

The casualties were dreadful, heads all mutilated, hands and feet torn off. The keys of the station ambulance were missing so Chris (Nicholson) and I fetched ours and made many horrible journeys with the living and the dying amid a haunting smell of burnt flesh.

On 1 January 1916 the FANY was authorised to drive ambulances for the British Army staffing convoys to Calais. Muriel recorded in her diary:

Jan 1st

We have started the first woman's M.A.C. (Motor Ambulance Convoy) ever to work for the British Army. Our camp is on a little hill near the sea, behind the Casino. Most of us live in tents and bathing machines. I share a small chalet with three others. The weather is fiendish, gales and torrents of rain. The cars are old and in a bad state, and we are short of drivers.

We mess in a big tent, all together. Lots of work but are all so very pleased to be here.

Jan 2nd

Got up at 5.45am and sat down for the first time, except for meals, at 7.30pm. We took over from the B.R.C. men yesterday. The cars stand in the open always, and the weather is awful. Suddenly word came that the Barges were there – every car goes at once, and the men are taken off to the hospitals.

These are bad cases, and one has to go very slowly.

Jan 14th

The Quarter-Master Sergeant tells us we are a great improvement on our predecessors! Last night we had a raging gale which howled over our little plateau and blew a tent right over. The unlucky possessions were blown all over the place. This morning all cars had to be at the Casino at 6am so we got up at 4.30am. The first lot of wounded arrived on the quay in pitch darkness. Calais is a healthy place.

I have lost the cough, and the pain in my back I had when we came here.

Jan 28th

Eighteen of us went to dine at the mess of a regiment which is here resting. They drank our health and cheered us; I had to reply for the Corps.

The winter of 1916/17 was hard. On very cold nights the FANYs had a night watch which stayed up all night and fired the engines of the cars every hour to keep them warm and ready for the morning's work. Those on night watch still had to do a full day's work. Muriel Thompson noted:

Feb 5th

Did night guard, cold awful. Cranked the Vulcan and three taxis every hour. Sat in cook-house and boiled water to thaw the petrol filters of the Napiers in the intervals. The filters were full of water from the petrol and were frozen solid nearly every time. Started day at 5 am and was about six hours on the quay. It snowed hard towards morning. We are consoled by hearing that everyone else has burst their radiators and some, their cylinders.

The girls are bricks, it is very hard work.

The FANYs lived in tents which were cold, wet, and alive with rats. The 'coffin cart' was an unpleasant aspect of the job, transporting bodies of soldiers found drowned in the canals and docks to the mortuary, and they witnessed horrors no less terrible than did the men:

April 25th

A terrible day. Were just starting for the evacuation when orders came to go at once, as fast as possible, to Audricq. I went, and three others. We went to the E.M.O.s and drew four stretchers, twelve blankets as usual, and four pillows for each car. We arrived at eleven; they never expected us so soon. It was terrible. Railway trucks full of burnt and blown up men. We took the fifteen worst. I helped with some of the stretchers. There were not enough bandages for all; their faces were skinless and awful. They were mad with pain, their puttees were charred and black, where they had any left. We got these poor awful things into the cars and started. One kept calling, 'Sister! Sister! I can't bear it, I can't bear it!' and then he broke off and began to try to sing with half his mouth gone. I was fortunate - my four were unconscious till we nearly reached Calais when they all began to cry out. I had an R.A.M.C. orderly with me. We drove those awful miles to Calais and luckily we could go at a fair pace as the road wasn't bad and there were no fractures. Got to the hospital and had our men taken out; one was dead. Returned to camp and I cried. Played four terrific sets of tennis in the middle of which we saw an aeroplane fall into the sea. The pilot was all right. Went to a concert at the Ordnance Place. After it was over we had coffee and sandwiches. I had prayed all the way to Audricq that my tyres should not puncture.

April 26th

The fourth man is dead, poor soul.

Muriel eventually served as second in command to Lilian Franklin for the Calais convoys and was further mentioned in dispatches on 9 April 1917.

On 1 January 1918 Muriel was appointed officer commanding the new FANY-VAD (Voluntary Aid Detachment) convoys based at St Omer and close to the front line. The St Omer convoy became part of the British Second Army on 4 May 1918 choosing a bright red fish as its official insignia in memory of the surgeon general's description of the corps in 1915, when still in conflict with British officialdom: 'They are neither fish, flesh nor fowl, but they are damn good red herrings'.

In spring 1918 the Germans launched a prolonged counter-offensive. During this period the St Omer convoys worked day and night.

Mar 29th

Another train from the Front in the middle of the night. We had our 31 cars out. Got back to bed at 5am. The news is terribly serious. Seventh day of the great offensive, we are just holding them. 10pm: I hear the troops marching along the Arques road singing 'Good-byeee' - poor boys. Now they are cheering.

April 9th

The most terrible bombardment has been going on all day. The guns have never ceased, though it is midnight as I write - we hear them very clearly and see the flashes in the sky.

April 10th

The 37th Division were entraining, it was a wonderful sight. These men had just come out of the Battle of Amiens for a few days of rest. They were lying down in their first deep sleep when the order came through for them to go into the line once more immediately, and there they were, marching away. As we got back to Camp the bombardment grew louder – it is terrible to think of what is happening a few miles away.

April 11th

All day the guns have been going furiously and all night. We have given a lot of ground and the Germans are in Armentières.

April 14th

The train got lost and we never started loading until 2.15am. We were repaid by a wonderful sight, first Lancers, then Artillery, then more Lancers, and then other Cavalry. They took over an hour to pass and looked splendid. The war is really coming home to one again as it never has since my first three months here in 1915.

April 15th

'Stand by for a T.A.T. (Temporary ambulance train) anytime between midnight and 3am,' comes the order to the Convoy, over the 'phone, and provision is made accordingly. The Cookhouse staff are warned for the nights are cold, and hot drinks will be in great request. The question of lamps is debated.

'May we use lamps?'

'No,' comes the stern reply. 'No lights allowed on cars.'

'But I saw a big car pass with a huge headlight just now,' argues the new arrival.

'Must have been a Staff car,' replies a senior. 'Then can't the Bosches see the Staff headlights...?' begins the innocent. She is told not to argue, and collapses wondering how on earth she is going to get round the twisty corners that lead to the C.C.S. without lights. The wise driver goes to bed, probably secures a useful spell of sleep before the call to action comes over the 'phone, for trains are more uncertain just now, and it will quite likely be three or four in the morning before the cars are wanted. At last the 'phone rings, the order comes, and every driver dashes out of bed, into her clothes, and off to her car, as fast as her legs will carry her. At the last moment side lights are allowed;

these are useful to avoid hitting other cars in the dark, but useless for seeing the road; so the ambulances file slowly out of the park, each with their little twinkly side lights, on and away over the lonely, deserted French roads, to the little station where the T.A.T.s come in. Londoners have seen the wounded arrive at Charing Cross, the police on guard, the arrival platform swept and garnished, the rows of beautiful cars each with its driver and orderly, the wounded men all nicely and tidily bandaged. When I see the T.A.T.s come in, the torn ragged blood-stained uniforms and utter, utter dead-beat appearance of the wounded men; the make-shift trucks in which they travel, their blood-stained bandages. The contrast. Tonight there is a shortage of stretcher bearers and one offers one's services in a temporary capacity. We look to the future and think, 'How long? How much longer must men be mangled, day in, day out?'

On 18 May the FANYs were called out following a heavy bombing raid on Arques and a huge ammunition dump. Halfway through their mission a second raid was launched with heavy salvos landing all around. The convoy staff were ordered to take cover but the women worked on regardless. For the unit's 'level-headed and stoic actions under such a prolonged and dangerous barrage' sixteen Military Medals were awarded and three Croix de Guerre.

Beryl Hutchinson describes their coolness under fire, and reveals Muriel's nickname!:

At the Veterinary Hospital next to the station, they had just loaded up the victims of the first wave of bombs trying for the railway line when another raid came over. The men had their orders to take shelter but the FANYs could not leave prostrate men unable to move so they put the ambulances in the deep shadow of one of the buildings and stayed with the men, chatting and smoking until the bombing was over. There was an Army ambulance with its driving cab, complete with driver, blown right off and four stretcher cases left inside.

They pulled up closely beside the wreck so the stretchers could be transferred. Noting that the spare wheel was still intact, they gave it shelter and ever after had two precious wheels for long runs. They got the Military Medal but we told them the citation was really for the theft of a spare wheel. 'Thompers' [Muriel] took three cars out to a French appeal and they were rewarded with the Croix de Guerre for their night's work. All the decorations were questioned as there were too many for one small unit but each one was so strongly supported for their cool example that all were allowed. There was no glamour in starting up engines but the girls said I should have been awarded a mangle handle rampant!

Muriel's medal collection resides at the National Army Museum in London.

After 11 November 1918 the FANY/VAD convoys were demobbed one by one. However, their skills were still in demand and many FANYs stayed in France and Belgium. They provided a Guard of Honour when the body of Edith Cavell, the heroic nurse executed by the Germans, was exhumed for reburial in England.

Badly affected by the death at Passchendaele in 1917 of her nephew Logie Colin Leggatt, a lieutenant in the Coldstream Guards, she was also exhausted after several years of continuous service. She returned to England on 2 September 1918.

After a month's recuperation, she joined the Women's Royal Air Force as a recruiting officer. She was finally demobilized on 1 October 1919. She resigned from the FANY in 1922 after a disagreement over the corps' post-war role.

Muriel does not appear to have returned to motor racing after the war. However, her ability with cars undoubtedly played a huge role in her life and made her a trail blazer at Brooklands and elsewhere.

A lifelong spinster, Muriel lived for the next two decades at her home in Kensington, dying on 3 March 1939 from 'sleeping sickness'. She was buried in Brompton cemetery in a family plot, her name inscribed in the stonework with the words 'She led a gallant life'.

Thompers will always have the notoriety that in 1917 she officially became the first woman to drive for the British army. Her own war diaries highlighted the horrors of war, but also the immense camaraderie and independence she experienced. It is perhaps somewhat of an omission that her grave makes no mention of the Military Medal.

Chapter 11

Gwenda Hawkes (1894-1990)

Women's Scottish Hospital Service in the First World War

Racing Car & Motorcycle record breaker

Gwenda Hawkes was born Gwenda Mary Glubb in 1894 in Fulwood, Lancashire, to Major General Sir Frederic Manley Glubb and Frances Letitia, née Bagot. Gwenda's father was an officer in the British Army who fought in the Boer Wars and became Chief Engineer of the British Second Army in the First World War. Her brother John was also a soldier who fought in the First World War and became known as 'Glubb Pasha' as commander of the Arab Legion from 1939 until 1956, 'pasha' being an Arabic title.

Gwenda was educated at Cheltenham Ladies' College and it was here that she taught herself to drive in a car belonging to the family of a school friend. She completed her education, as did many young ladies of the day, in Paris and became a fluent French speaker.

When the First World War broke out, Gwenda joined the Scottish Women's Hospitals organisation as a volunteer. The SWH for Foreign Service (which existed between 1914 and 1919) was part of the women's suffrage response to the First World War. By June 1915 the SWH had responsibility for more than 1,000 beds with 250 staff including 19 female doctors. By the end of the war there were fourteen Scottish Women's Hospitals in France, Serbia, Russia, Salonica and Macedonia.

Gwenda was posted to the Crimea. The train journey to her deployment took several arduous weeks with the occupants having to get out and chop wood for the engine every twenty miles or so. Gwenda was involved in the Dobruja Retreat in 1916, in which Bulgaria, as part of the Central Powers, overran this part of Romania that was allied with Russia and France. She was mentioned in dispatches, apparently for making emergency repairs to her ambulance under fire. She would eventually be awarded the British War

Medal and the Victory Medal, and the Cross of St George and St Stanislav by the Romanian government.

By 1918 she had become an assistant administrator of the WRAF, and on 1 July 1919 she became the Deputy Administrator. However, her tenure ended in scandal. In a power struggle with the male dominated establishment, the administrative head of the WRAF, Violet Blanche Douglas-Pennant, was sacked for not controlling the discipline of some of her subordinates. In fighting for her position, Violet accused Gwenda of having an affair with an army officer, Colonel Sam Janson. His landlady claimed she saw Gwenda leave his room and found her hot water bottle in Janson's bed. Gwenda said she had given Janson her hot bottle as he had a recurrence of 'trench fever' and she had entered the room in the morning to take his temperature. Gwenda was even examined by a doctor who concluded, 'There is no definite physical sign of virginity, but I am of the opinion that there has never been penetration of this girl.' The *London Evening Standard* reported the 'cruel and wicked charges that put a girl's honour at stake'.

Gwenda married Colonel Janson, who was by then London manager for the Spyker Car Company, on 17 February 1920 at Holy Trinity, Brompton.

Perhaps missing the excitement that the Great War had brought, Gwenda became interested in motorcycle racing and began competing in events at Brooklands. Also, in November 1921, she established the 1,000-mile record on a Ner-A-Car motorcycle on behalf of Australian businessman S.F. Edge. Achieving daily runs of 190 miles she completed the 1,000 miles on icy roads without any accidents or breakdowns. She also completed a non-stop ride of three hundred miles. In 1922 she took the Double-12-hour record at Brooklands on a Trump-JAP, over two periods of twelve hours as twenty-four-hour racing was banned at Brooklands. While she rode the motorcycle, S.F. Edge drove a Spyker C4 car, also setting a record.

Gwenda spent a considerable amount of time away from home participating in events on behalf of Trump Motorcycles of Byfleet. As a result, a close relationship developed between Gwenda and Colonel Neil Stewart, a keen rider himself and director of Trump who accompanied her and acted as her mechanic. Perhaps as a consequence of this, Colonel Janson divorced her in 1923. She married Neil Stewart and they went on an adventurous honeymoon in North America, sailing down the Yukon River on a raft with a cabin they built themselves, living off the land, hunting, fishing and foraging.

During the last months of winter they stayed at a mission inside the Arctic Circle where they earned their keep by shooting game for the kitchen, and then returned to civilisation with a dog sled team.

They returned to Europe for the 1924 season and moved to France to take advantage of the brand new, banked, oval race circuit at Montlhéry near Paris, where there was no time restriction as at Brooklands. At Montlhéry Gwenda broke the world 24-hour motorcycle speed record on a Terrot-JAP. In 1925 she and her husband broke twenty-one long-distance records using a 346cc Rudge. They achieved one record by riding two hours on, two hours off, lapping at a constant 1 minute 40 seconds. They also set a new track record of 54.21 mph. Gwenda preferred setting records over racing.

Later she crashed at 90 mph on a Clément Gladiator motorcycle. Initially she was thought to be dead. She in fact suffered a fractured skull and multiple other injuries. It took her some months and much pain to recover. When she recovered, she and her husband crossed the North Sea from Aberdeen to Stavanger in an open motor boat.

In 1928 she began riding for motorcycle manufacturer Douglas Hawkes, who owned the Derby engine and car company and produced motorcycles under the brand Brooklands Engineering Works. For him she drove a Vernon-Derby light-weight racing car breaking more records, and in 1929 she set several records with co-driver (and fellow Motorsport Military Hero) 'Sammy' Davis. In 1930 she was hired by Austin to regain a Montlhéry speed record recently taken by MG. She succeeded and took five other records at the same time.

Following these successes, Douglas Hawkes imported a Miller Special car from the USA which he customised. In this she also reached a top speed of 140 mph at speed trials at Arpajon in France before the engine blew up.

She also rode a Hawkes-Stewart cyclecar setting records with it; she eventually set fifty records in two classes of three-wheel cyclecars.

In October 1930 Hawkes increased the engine size to 2.0 litres in the Miller, renaming it the 'Derby-Miller'. Despite high winds, and wearing the front tyres through to their inner canvas, she managed to break the 100 km record; and in early 1931 she set a new 10-mile speed record, achieving 137.2 mph in the Derby-Miller.

She was elected an honorary member of the British Racing Driver's Club (BRDC), and at the Paris Motor Show she was presented with the Montlhéry

Challenge Trophy for her record attempts at the auto drome. In France she was known as the 'reigning queen of Montlhéry'.

Continuing to set records, in 1933 she narrowly avoided disaster when during a high-speed run her helmet blew down over her eyes, blinding her. For some reason she was unable to push it back up. Luckily, however, she was on a straight and brought the car to a controlled stop. On another occasion a nut on a carburettor float chamber came loose, detaching the cover and spraying fuel into Gwenda's face at 140 mph; she opened her mouth at the wrong time and swallowed a mouthful of fuel, alcohol and oil.

The year 1934 saw a change in her fortunes. In June she was forced to retire early from the Le Mans 24 Hour race. Then after competing in the Monto Carlo Rally she decided never to enter a rally again. In early 1935 she was injured in a skiing accident. Recovering, she entered Le Mans again, but retired without completing the race. At the Grand Prix of Dieppe in July she retired after one lap with clutch failure. Then at the Grand Prix de Berne in August she finished last having been lapped several times.

Over the August bank holiday of 1935 a duel took place at Brooklands between Gwenda and female rival Kay Petre, in 'a match race to set records'. Gwenda set out on a preliminary warm-up in a car set up for the smooth Montlhéry track and hit the notorious 'Brooklands bump' on the rougher UK oval. The car took off and flew through the air before crashing down on the front axle. She was unharmed however, and over that weekend the two women exchanged higher and higher speeds. The race officials became concerned about the rivalry between the two, and insisted they make separate runs. At one point Gwenda's exhaust silencer exploded, almost asphyxiating her with fumes entering the cockpit of the car. Finally Gwenda went out and became the fastest woman ever at Brooklands, with a lap speed of 135.95 miles per hour, beating the record set by Kay Petre the previous day.

In February 1936 the BARC removed its restrictions and allowed women to race under the same conditions as men. In September Gwenda entered two mixed BRDC driver events, but she failed to finish either due to mechanical issues. She raced in another mixed driver event in September 1937, the BRDC 500 mile at Brooklands, with George Duller in a Duesenberg; they came seventh in a field of twenty-two.

Gwenda continued as a test driver for Hawkes and their working relationship became a full-blown affair. She divorced Neil Stewart and married Douglas

Hawkes in 1937. She was 42 and still breaking speed records; now she had broken her second marriage.

In the Second World War Mr and Mrs Hawkes worked together at the Brooklands Engineering Company, where they made armaments and Gwenda became a skilled lathe operator. She also returned to volunteer ambulance driving work.

After the war they sailed in the Aegean and Mediterranean on their yacht *Elpis* and spent time on the island of Poros. She remained an avid traveller all her life. Douglas Hawkes died in 1974, Gwenda on 27 May 1990 aged 95.

In 1930 *The Citizen* described Gwenda as 'the most unassuming woman, and although a famous racing motorist, she hates publicity'. An article in *Sports Illustrated* of 1958 noted, 'Records to her were cold facts, with no regard to sex. They could be challenged alone on the track.' 'Sammy' Davis described her as 'the greatest woman driver of her time'.

One wonders where she might have been in motorsport if she had been born a century later. Despite the lack of other female competitors, Gwenda and her contemporaries, such as Kay Petre, were written about often in newspapers and magazines. Most articles recounted the sheer number of records broken by Gwenda Hawkes, however some were rather probing into her personal life. That is most likely why she hated public attention. For Gwenda, the focus was on speed and the records she could achieve and not impressing the media.

Chapter 12

Captain Robert Benoist (1895-1944)

L'Armée de l'Air in the First World War

SOE agent in the Second World War

Racing car driver

Robert Marcel Charles Benoist was born on 20 March 1895 near Rambouillet. He grew up alongside a generation of the Rothschild family in idyllic surroundings outside Paris. Baroness Charlotte de Rothschild employed Robert Benoist's grandfather as her steward at the Abbaye des Vaux de Cernay. Robert's father, Gaston, known as Georges, also took a role also in service to this wealthiest of families. Baron Henri de Rothschild was the same age as Georges and they married and had children at roughly the same time. Robert Benoist and his older brother Maurice grew up alongside James and Phillippe Rothschild. Robert, a lifelong seeker of adventure, had become an accomplished hunter before he was 10, demonstrating it to all by shooting a hare outside the dining room window.

When Robert was a teenager, Georges decided to leave the Rothschild's employment and set up his own kennels for hunting dogs. Robert and Maurice would have seen their former playmates drive expensive cars while they had to make do with bicycles. Nevertheless, Robert joined the Versailles Cycling Club, and won several races. At 18 he left school and began to work towards his dreams by getting a job in a garage in Versailles.

In the summer of 1913 Robert and some of his friends from the cycling club rode to Amiens to watch the Grand Prix de l'Automobile Club de France. The group camped out on one of the sharp corners of the circuit in the village of Moreuil to have a prime viewing position for the eight-hour race. The race was won by Peugeot, but Delage, who would become pivotal in Benoist's racing career, came close. Benoist returned home telling all who would listen that he would one day race for Delage.

From the garage in Versailles, Robert moved on to Jean-Albert Gregoire's Automobile Company in Poissy, and then to Unic in Puteaux, with each move getting physically closer to the Delage factory in Courbevoie.

However, it was now August 1914 and France and Germany went to war. Initially he was not called up, as Unic were building military trucks. But in August 1915 he was sent to St Avold airfield near Bourges to become a pilot in the newly formed L' Armée de l'Air. To Benoist this was an exciting adventure. He qualified as a pilot in November 1915, and in April 1916 was deployed to the 50ème Escadrille at Vaubercourt near Verdun. From there he flew reconnaissance missions for the artillery.

Benoist flew with an observer called Lt Georges Domino. Sometimes they took handheld bombs with them, but usually they were only armed with pistols. In November 1916 he received a commendation for intercepting some German planes attacking a fellow pilot and scaring them off. In May 1917 Benoist and Domino were given one of the new Morane-Parasol monoplanes equipped with a Lewis gun. They shot down their first German plane over the Argonne. Two days later they were themselves shot down by groundfire. Benoist crash-landed in no mans' land and together they crawled through the mud back to the French trenches.

But Benoist would never again be an active fighter pilot. Instead he was transferred to fighter training school near Senlis. In November 1917 he was posted to 463ème Escadrille flying patrols over Parisian airspace. In March 1918 he was posted to the aerobatic school at Pont Long near Pau where he saw his war out as an instructor.

He stayed in the Armée de l'Air until September 1919, after which for eighteen months he failed to find a job. He did not want to return to being a mechanic, he wanted to be a racing driver. He wrote to all the major car manufacturers in France offering his services as a test racing driver, and in early 1921 received a reply from a little-known marque called De Marcay who had a factory on the Avenue de Suffren in Paris. They had been manufacturing aircraft in the war, but now they produced an 1,100cc cyclecar and wanted someone to test it. It was the opportunity he had been waiting for, and soon found himself conducting test runs through the streets of the École Militaire district of Paris.

Benoist made his racing debut in the summer of 1921 entering the Paris to Nice trial, a test of endurance for both car and driver. He finished eighth, which attracted the attention of a company called Société des Moteurs

Salmson. Salmson had also diversified into automotive manufacturing from aero-engine construction during the war, and were developing their own designs. Perhaps prompted by their aerospace experience, they chose to recruit former pilots to test drive for them. Robert Benoist was signed with two other former Armée de l'Air pilots.

Now aged 27 and with some financial security, he was able to marry his girlfriend Paule Ajustron from Toulouse. They settled in the Rue Ordener, near the Sacré-Coeur basilica, and a daughter was born, Jacqueline.

Benoist became the lead cyclecar driver for Salmson following the death of a teammate in early 1922, and went on to make his international debut in August competing at Brooklands. In 1922 he achieved three victories: Brooklands, Le Mans and Tarragona. In 1923 he won the Bol d'Or in France and became the star of the Salmson team.

But behind the scenes all was not well at the company. The head of sales, André Lombard, who provided the impetus to go racing, had fallen out with the head of engineering, Emile Petit. Someone had to go, and it was decided that it was better to retain the mechanical expertise, so Lombard was fired. Sales duly dropped, and it was decided that there were better and cheaper ways to advertise than to race.

Meanwhile, Delage decided that they needed to do something about their Grand Prix performance, having lost out to Duesenberg in 1921 and Fiat in 1922. Despite significant investment in development, they again lost out in 1923, this time to Britain's Sunbeam and legendary driver Major Henry Segrave. Delage approached Benoist, for whom this was a dream come true. Chief engineer Albert Lory at Delage was in charge of race development at Salmson when Benoist drove for them, and he and Benoist had developed a friendship. When Delage were looking for a competitive driver it was Lory who advised them to approach Benoist.

Delage's existing number one driver was Réné Thomas, a one-time aviator and major star in motor racing, but aging. He took Benoist under his wing, coaching him through the spring of 1924, during which they won some events and set some hill-climb records. In August 1924 Delage were ready for the Grand Prix de l'ACF at Lyons, a fourteen-mile circuit on public highways.

Twenty-two cars entered the race, including Fiat, Alfa Romeo, Bugatti, Delage and Sunbeam, and an illustrious line-up of drivers including Ascari, Campari, Kenelm Guinness, Henry Segrave and Enzo Ferrari. Benoist was now racing in the big league, and he came third.

He then entered the St Sebastian Grand Prix in Spain in September, but crashed out, unhurt, after five laps. He was disappointed when Delage decided not to compete in October in the Italian Grand Prix.

In the 1925 season the first race was at Spa in Belgium. Only seven cars began the race. Benoist was forced to retire due to a broken fuel tank.

The next race was at Montlhéry with a much bigger field. But it was raining and tragedy struck: Ascari spun off in a high-speed left hander, the car cartwheeled ejecting him, and then landed on him. He died on the way to hospital. Alfa retired from the event, leaving the Delage car piloted by Benoist and teammate Alberto Divo to take the win. This was the first win by a French driver since 1913. Benoist received his trophy from President Gaston Doumergue. The bouquet he was awarded he placed at the site of Ascari's crash.

Delage didn't attend the next race in Italy, where Nuvolari, Ascari's replacement, escaped with his life from a serious crash. The only real competition was the American Duesenberg team, which had won at Indianapolis. Alfa Romeo won the 1925 season but withdrew from the sport before the season's end, leaving Delage to dominate in the last race in Spain. But one of their four drivers, Paul Torchy, died, and Benoist retired with a mechanical defect.

In 1926 Benoist won the Mont Angel hill climb; when close to the finish line he spun his car, and instead of trying to turn it around he engaged reverse and crossed the line backwards. This highlighted his quick thinking that would become crucial as he entered a new world a dozen years later, when recruited to the British Special Operations Executive.

The new Delage 15S8 arrived in time for the 1926 season and its debut was at St Sebastian. But the exhaust pipes passed too close to the cockpit and each driver had to retire with heat exhaustion. Benoist fainted when he got out of the car. They tried again at Brooklands with the same result. Louis Delage refused to enter the race at Monza.

The problem was cured in 1927 by re-routing the exhaust system, and the car became extraordinarily quick. Benoist returned to multiple hill-climb wins and won the first non-championship Grand Prix at Montlhéry lapping the rest of the field three times over thirty laps. The Delage cars were so fast that at the official ACF race at Montlhéry in July, Bugatti withdrew their cars to avoid inevitable humiliation. Delage completed a 1-2-3 in the race with Benoist on the top step. Benoist won four of the five Grands Prix that year and at the end of the season was declared 'world champion' by the French press. At the end of 1927 he was made a Chevalier de la Légion d'Honneur. For a humble gamekeeper's son, he had done well.

The economics of racing were, however, too draining on the Delage accounts, and the decision was taken not to compete in 1928. Jobs were scarce – Bugatti were the only real entrants, racing against their own customers. So Benoist took a position as sales manager at the Parisian 'Garage Banville', which was more of a social club than a garage, for the wealthy and their expensive cars. On the ground floor was a spacious hall for car sales, below it a service department. Above it were six floors with a double-width winding car ramp with space for 600 cars. On the sixth floor was a pitch-and-putt course and a driving range, there were three indoor tennis courts, a gymnasium and a restaurant. Partly due to Benoist's influence, an extraordinary promotional event took place: a hill climb using the winding ramp. The garage quickly became a hub for the racing community of Paris.

Benoist entered the Le Mans 24 hours in 1928 coming 8th, and raced for Bugatti at St Sebastian, but otherwise he didn't race Grand Prix again for over five years, throwing himself fully into the activities of Garage Banville.

In 1932 Benoist was offered a job as a development driver for Bugatti, and in 1934, having served out his notice from Garage Banville, he became a full-time Bugatti employee. But the 1934 season would be ultra-competitive with the German government supporting the entry of Mercedes, and Benoist and Jean Bugatti were forced to conclude they didn't have the resources to be competitive in Grand Prix. They chose to focus their efforts solely on Le Mans.

Their 1936 attempt was thwarted by industrial unrest. In 1937 there was a hideous seven car pile-up that resulted in two drivers being killed. Eventually Benoist (himself driving) took the win with co-driver Jean-Pierre Wimille, driving 2,043 miles, over 90 miles more than the previous record. This put Bugatti back on the map.

Benoist was now 42 years old and it was time to retire from racing. He continued to manage the Bugatti showroom and the competition department.

The Munich Crisis of September 1938 forced France to call up their reserve military officers with Benoist ordered to report to Toulon and a return to the L'Armée de l'Air. But the tension eased and he was demobilised late in 1938. He returned to Bugatti and managed the win at Le Mans in 1939, but almost immediately he was returned again to uniform.

Despite tensions in Europe, competition development continued at Bugatti which resulted in the death in a testing accident of Jean Bugatti, heir to the Bugatti empire. His father Ettore was devastated. Ettore, in the wake of this tragedy, at least managed the relocation of his motor works away from Molsheim in Alsace and near Germany, to Bordeaux due to the instability in Europe. In September 1939 war began and everyone's lives changed forever. France was invaded, the British Expeditionary Force was trapped at Dunkirk and the Germans had simply advanced around the Maginot Line to enter France.

He was given orders to leave the airfield at Le Bourget and report to Blois, and then to an airfield at Tarbes near the Pyrenees. To get there he was given permission to use a Bugatti type 57 supercharged sports car. It was June 1940 and on the way he was intercepted by German forces. But before they could take him into captivity, he took his chance and made a break for it, speeding off along a sideroad. He headed for the country house of a friend and hid the car in a barn. Benoist was forced to ditch his uniform and he returned to Paris and worked for Bugatti, whose industrial capacity had already suffered. Benoist hated being under occupation, but at that point there was no resistance movement to join.

Over in the UK, former motor racing rival Willy Grover-Williams had enlisted in the British Army. Having being one of those who had escaped from Dunkirk, he was desperate for action, so he joined the Special Operations Executive (SOE), Churchill's organisation designed to 'set Europe ablaze' under German occupation. The SOE was an all-volunteer force formed to conduct sabotage, guerrilla warfare, and espionage missions with resistance forces across Europe and the Far East. Willy had spent much time in France as a racing driver, spoke fluent French, and knew France, especially Paris. His first mission was to return to Paris and set up a clandestine network of operatives. It was May 1942. To do this he first assessed all his pre-war French contacts and his first choice was garage owner Albert Fremont whom he had known since the early 1930s. He called at Fremont's garage to approach him about working for the British in organising disruption and sabotage. Fremont enthusiastically agreed and they began discussing others in Paris who could join. The first name that came up was Robert Benoist, with whom Fremont had served in the L'Armée de l'Air years before.

Benoist agreed immediately. He had already become active in 'Action Vengeance', an organisation to help people get out of occupied France. He had the advantage that his work with Bugatti allowed him to travel freely around France. Ettore Bugatti had no desire to help the Germans and he helped Benoist with the documents he needed.

Benoist began recruiting amongst his social circle almost straight away, although not all met the approval of his SOE boss. For example, Willy had no confidence in racing driver Jean-Pierre Wimille.

By now Robert had split from his wife Paule and was now living with his brother Maurice on the Boulevard Berthier. Maurice was recruited by Robert without any consultation with his SOE masters as he trusted his older brother.

Their first success was to create a sabotage network inside the Citroën factory who were operating for the Germans. But it wasn't until March 1943 that the network created by Willy, Benoist and Fremont, named the 'Chestnut' network, received their first parachute drop of weapons. It was made in woods near Rambouillet, Benoist's childhood village. He knew the woods and owned a house and some woodland nearby. He also ran a transportation business from there. Benoist's additional vehicles were a great help. They waited for the coded broadcasts from the BBC world service around 9.15 pm and then awaited the drop at about 1 am. At the landing zone as they heard the plane overhead they illuminated torches in their clearing. Following the drop, the three men had four containers to collect and it was crucial to locate them all so as to not compromise their local operation. Their first haul contained Sten guns, Mills and gammon grenades, medical supplies, explosives, detonators, medical supplies and identification armbands for when the uprising began. Luxury items were included too, such as cigarettes, chocolate and tinned fruit. For the next parachute they took Maurice along too. Benoist's home in the woods became a store, and he built a false wall to deceive inspections.

In the summer of 1943, the skills of both Willy and Benoist came in useful when they were tasked with driving an SOE agent, Richard Heslop, from the village of Marce to Paris. Heslop had two radio transmitters for the Chestnut network. He was surprised by how quickly they had made the journey in their Bugatti car, and how easily they bluffed their way through a German roadblock.

A shattering event of that summer was the collapse of an SOE network called 'Prosper'. One fugitive of that was the tenacious agent Noor Inayat Khan, who had already shot her way out of trouble once. Chestnut operatives under Willy's guidance sheltered Noor and France Antelme, a senior British

SOE officer with extensive knowledge of the networks. He had to be evacuated back to the UK and kept safe in the meantime. Under Willy's orders, Maurice collected the fugitives from an apartment in Paris and took them back to his own, where Willy and Robert joined them for dinner. Robert offered them sanctuary in his mistress's apartment near the École Militaire, where they stayed until the group moved to Robert's country house in the woods near Auffargis. The plan was for Antelme to fly out on an SOE infiltration aircraft on 17 July, but the rendezvous was missed, so Robert took them back to Paris where they made separate departures by train. Noor left for Neuilly-sur-Seine out of central Paris while Antelme headed for Tours. Antelme was captured but said nothing under questioning. Sadly, he was deported to a concentration camp in Poland and executed in 1945.

One of the primary reasons for Noor's success as a radio operator was her cunning and professionalism for always being on the move and not transmitting from the same place. The Germans could trace the transmissions and could also create false messaging with captured radios. Roland Dowlen was an SOE Chestnut radio operator. As an introvert, he had perhaps been complacent in not using distant enough venues for his radio operations, leading the Germans to put one of his locations under surveillance. In late July four cars arrived full of Germans and raided the house. There was an exchange of gunfire and he was led away by the SD to their notorious Avenue Foch headquarters. Word spread quickly and Willy, Maurice and his wife Suzy took shelter at the house in the woods. Robert had been warned to stay away.

Two days later on Monday 2 August Maurice went to his apartment and was arrested. His interrogator asked where Robert could be found.

The SD police arrived at the Benoist house in Auffargis two hours after Maurice's arrest. Willy Grover-Williams was detained and beaten for information but gave nothing away to 'Monsieur Jean', a Spanish thug in the employ of the Germans. Maurice was then brought to the family home as his parents were being interrogated by Jean. It took eight hours before Robert's father Georges finally gave in and said where the resistance arms caches were. Maurice and Willy were imprisoned at the Avenue Foch. Maurice survived the war, but his integrity was tarnished. Some believe he betrayed the Chestnut network.

Maurice later claimed they clearly knew about some of the structure of Chestnut. He also said that they had a map that indicated Robert's country house on it. During post-war enquiries Maurice Benoist seemed to try to claim that Roland Dowlen had cracked and given up intelligence, but all of this is disputed. If he had, it seems he would have at least lasted the standard 48 hours to give his cell the chance of escape.

Robert Benoist had been out and about in Paris. Telephoning his brother's apartment he spoke to a man with a German accent. He instantly guessed there had been a betrayal. Enquiries he made confirmed it. He spoke to his sister-in-law Suzy, Maurice's wife, who had been released after 48 hours. She asked to meet him and he suspected it was a trap. He went to a post office phone to try to discover what had happened to his parents, but Germans at the telephone exchange were onto him. He fled the post office but was spotted by SD officers in a car. He was bundled into the back of the car, hemmed in by men either side of him.

In the car, a Hotchkiss, he discovered he could reach the extended leather straps that opened the rear doors. On the Rue de Richelieu, Benoist seized his chance and pulled on a strap and heaved both himself and one of the Germans out onto the road. The German broke his fall as they hit the cobblestones and Benoist took off into the back streets. Eventually he found sanctuary and made contact with an SOE contact, and two weeks later he embarked on his escape journey. He travelled 200 miles by train to Angers, then to the village of Briollay, and from there to his map reference rendezvous to fly out. At that rural location he was surprised to see a gathering of famed SOE agents and leaders of resistance and escape networks. After clearing the landing strip of wandering cattle, the Hudson plane landed in mist, one agent got out and then Benoist and nine others boarded for evacuation. Landing at RAF Tangmere, the agents were transferred to London for debriefing.

The authorities, satisfied with his allegiances, granted him a period of freedom. He then completed a training course for returning SOE agents and a three-week course on explosives. Next he was given an emergency commission on the British Army general list, and in early October, aged 47, he began briefing for his return mission, which was to conduct a demolition of electricity supplies near Nantes. He would be based in Nantes and try to take over what was left of the old Chestnut network under the new name of 'Clergyman'. His new pseudonym would be Roger Bremontier (same initials). His codename was 'Lionel'.

Meanwhile Robert's brother Maurice, having got his parents and wife released from custody, was helping the SD dismantle the Chestnut network. Joe Saward's excellent book *Grand Prix Saboteurs* shows he was probably a great source of information for the Germans. He also tried to betray Noor Inayat Khan on several occasions.

The Clergyman network had four roles: receive arms and explosives, attack electricity pylons around the Loire, prepare for attacks on railways around Nantes, and to try to prevent the Germans destroying Nantes in a retreat. In October 1943 Benoist touched down at a secret airfield near Soucelles in the Loire. Once the agents had dispersed and hidden their equipment, Benoist and a man called Henri Déricourt made their way to Paris. Déricourt was a double agent. In Paris, Robert began contacting those left from Chestnut. One of them confirmed that Maurice had been the traitor.

Robert Benoist returned to Soucelles to retrieve equipment before heading to Nantes to establish Clergyman. He then joined two others in a Benoist Citroën truck carrying gas bottles to disguise their illicit supplies. A German policeman stopped them, thinking they were black-marketeers, and took them to police headquarters in Robert's truck. Robert had said he'd travel in the back, and on the way he dropped off the truck with as much equipment as he could, then stole a bicycle, fled to his house in Auffargis and holed up for several days. The other two escaped from the German HQ as they arrived. Robert had lost a suitcase of clothes and other effects marked RB, which were identified as his by his brother Maurice. As most of his papers had been captured, 'Roger Bremontier' was now compromised.

The Clergyman plans were unravelling, and to make matters worse his radio operator was captured, leaving Robert no communication to London. But he decided to press on with developing the Nantes network before returning to London. Back in England, Robert was interviewed twice by MI5, mainly about his brother Maurice.

Robert Benoist then returned again to France under a new name, Daniel Perdrige, with radio operator Denise Bloch. His new mission was to attack the electricity supply for Nantes. They were landed by Lysander light infiltration aircraft on 2 March 1944 south-west of Paris. In the city Robert made contact with his treacherous brother to get hold of a vehicle to travel to Nantes. He was certain Maurice would never give him up.

On 16 May he and his crew accomplished their mission, the demolition of electricity pylons supplying Nantes. It took the Germans seven days to restore the power. Then four days later Benoist and his crew did it again.

On 1 June 1944 the first BBC D-Day code was broadcast that put the Clergyman teams on standby. On the evening of 5 June the invasion message was broadcast. That night Clergyman and other groups went into action on telephone lines, railways, felling trees onto roads and blowing up bridges. By mid-June, after the Allies had established their Normandy bridgehead, Robert Benoist returned with Denise to Paris to visit his 68-year-old mother. Jeanne died before he could make it to her bedside. The interrogation in the previous year had fatally weakened her.

Robert then made for a safe-house in Rue Fustel de Coulanges in Montparnasse. He knocked quietly and when it opened he found himself looking into the barrel of a pistol. Neither Robert nor Denise were armed. They were led up to the ransacked apartment where four SS officers were waiting.

Handcuffed, Robert asked to use the toilet, where he managed to free himself from one cuff. He tried to escape out of the window but the SS broke in and dragged him back through the window. He and Denise were taken to the SD building in the Avenue Foch. Robert was questioned every day for a month.

On 8 August Robert was taken from his cell ready for the move to Germany. With him were his radio operator Denise Bloch and Violette Szabo. On the train were several other SOE agents and resistance members. The men were taken to Neue Bremm torture camp, the females were taken to Ravensbrücke.

After three nights at Neue Bremm they were transported in railway trucks to Buchenwald labour camp. Benoist wanted to escape, so much so that he attacked those who did not.

Thirty-seven men described as the 'Robert Benoist group' by the authorities were the SOE agents who entered Buchenwald on 27 August 1944. Only five would survive. On Saturday, 9 September, Robert and fifteen others were summoned across the personal address system to report for 'special treatment'. Polish orderlies reported on Monday 11th that the sixteen were still alive but had been badly beaten. By Monday night they were dead, having been executed by slow strangulation. Willy Grover-Williams survived until 23 March 1945 when he was either shot or strangled.

After the German surrender, a memorial service was held at the church of St Pierre in Neuilly-sur-Seine in memory of Robert Benoist. Paris's first post-war motor race was held on a circuit commencing in the Bois de Boulogne. It was called the 'Coupe Robert Benoist'. At the end of the race the engines fell silent, the Last Post was sounded, and a bouquet of flowers was presented to Benoist's daughter Jacqueline Garnier.

Benoist was mentioned in dispatches in November 1945 as citations and awards were decided upon for the hundreds of SOE agents who lost their lives; and Captain Robert Benoist is recorded on the Brookwood Memorial in Surrey. The French motor racing fraternity named several monuments after him; a huge concrete spectator stand at the Reims-Gueux Circuit was named in honour of this heroic son of France and bears his name in faded paint.

One of France's greatest sons, and arguably France's first motor racing world champion, he had thrown his all into becoming a racing driver, but twice gave his all and ultimately his life in the cause of the liberation of his country, with total commitment and without fear.

Chapter 13

Flight Lieutenant Raymond Baxter (1922-2006)

RAF, twice mentioned in dispatches in the Second World War

Motorsport commentator, TV presenter & rally driver

Raymond Frederic Baxter was born and raised in Ilford in East London. He revered his father, who was a teacher and was most likely responsible for Raymond's lifelong passion for motorcars. He adored his mother and was desolate with grief when she died of flu during an epidemic in 1933.

When Raymond was a small child his father built him a car which he pedalled around the blocks near his home in Wellesley Road, Ilford – at that time the streets were almost devoid of cars. By his account, he pushed it to its limits but never managed to overturn it, although he did fell a large pedestrian by taking his legs from under him after rounding a blind corner.

Like many other boys of his time, he thrived on the creative mechanics of Meccano; he had a methylated-spirits-driven train set; and he would visit Croydon airport with an uncle to watch the planes coming in.

He attended Christchurch Road Elementary and then Ilford County High School. One of his passions was singing, and in 1934 he won a silver medal at the Barking Music Festival. He also boxed, acted with aplomb in school plays, and played the violin in the orchestra. He sprinted at county standard, and once raced against some visiting German pupils. His words on their visit: 'War was inevitable, and these blond, handsome boys certainly had the swagger typical of the Hitler Youth of the day.' One wonders whether he later faced them in aerial combat. He witnessed the violence of Oswald Moseley's fascists as they battled the police and their communist opponents in the East End.

He drove cars at 15 and clocked up hundreds of miles on his bicycle. He also enjoyed fell walking and climbing.

An early disaster was when he was caught smoking at school and the harsh disciplinarian headmaster expelled him in spite of pleas from other masters at the school. It crushed one of Raymond's main dreams – RADA (the Royal Academy of Dramatic Arts). He left school with a smattering of qualifications including a distinction in English but flunked the civil service exam.

Raymond then worked briefly at Hampton's furniture store near Trafalgar Square and then with the Water Board. On 3 September 1939 he was sailing at Walton-on-the-Naze when he heard his first air-raid warning of the war.

Raymond immediately joined the Local Defence Volunteers (later the Home Guard), and did night duty defending the Water Board installation on the edge of Wanstead Park, in uniform, armed with a .303 Lee Enfield with a single magazine of five rounds. One night to keep himself awake he practised a 'for inspection, port arms': pulling back the bolt to show the breach was clear. However, he forgot he had a live magazine attached and when he 'eased springs' he accidentally fired off a round. Reinforcements came running, but he didn't get into trouble.

What Raymond really wanted was to join the RAF, and as soon as he was 17 years and 9 months he applied to the Air Crew Receiving Centre in St John's Wood. He was then transferred to Initial Training in Torquay. After six weeks he passed out as a leading aircraftsman. Then, along with fellow recruits, he boarded a ship in Scotland and set sail under Royal Navy escort for Canada en route for flight training in Oklahoma.

Raymond achieved the distinction of being the first on his course to fly solo, having recorded a total of six hours and fifty-five minutes in the air. The pilots were also taught navigation, night flying and blind-instrument flying.

While in the USA Raymond experienced his first taste of broadcasting when invited to speak on local radio in Pittsburg, Kansas. The owner of the radio station offered him a job if he ever came back.

During a period of leave Raymond took a Greyhound bus to New Orleans to see Louis Armstrong. Not only did he get to see him, he also met him and shook his hand:

'I've travelled over four thousand miles for this,' said Raymond.

'Well, thank you,' replied Satchmo, 'and good luck.'

The final part of his training was to recover from a spin under the scrutiny of the RAF Wing Commander. This was forbidden under US flight training but a necessity for the British. He passed.

In May 1942 it was time for the journey home. After a brief period of leave Raymond attended No 5 Advanced Flying Unit in Shropshire. On 18 July 1942 he was strapped into a Hurricane. After completing a series of flight drills, including two landings and an overshoot, his logbook was signed off. This was the only time he flew a Hurricane.

On 4 August 1942 at Hawarden in Cheshire, Raymond flew his first Spitfire. When he 'opened the taps' for the first time, 'a single expletive shot through my brain and out of my lips, though not blasphemous, it was a cry of pure joy and ecstasy.'

He was then posted to No 65 (East India) Squadron, part of 11 Group. After a spell in front line operations, No 65 was posted to Drem in East Lothian for 'in rest' operations. For Raymond this included readiness drills, stand-bys, convoy escorts and anti-intruder patrols. On one occasion in poor visibility he was fired on by a Royal Navy battleship.

Early in 1943 he volunteered and found himself posted to No 93 Squadron in North Africa. His accommodation was a ridge tent dug four feet into the ground near aircraft dispersal shared with three others. Ammo boxes made good poker tables. Raymond flew with 93 for nine months during which time his logbook records active service in North Africa, Malta, Sicily, Salerno, and Naples. In the invasion of Sicily he witnessed the horror of gliders ditching in the sea short of the island. Operations in support of the invasion were made more complex by the distance of flying from Malta and the restrictions on fuel. Raymond had one close call flying back after extended combat against the Luftwaffe when he landed with only four gallons of fuel left. He recorded verified kills during these sorties.

Raymond, or 'Bax' as he had become known, had complete confidence in the Spitfire. Once when returning to Malta he could only get one wheel down, and once down he could not get it up again. Flight control suggested he fly out to sea and bale out, but he didn't want to lose an aircraft and felt he'd seen too many bale-outs go wrong. In the end he landed on one wheel with only minor damage to the wing tip and propeller.

During the invasion of Salerno, Raymond's squadron was given orders to chase enemy aircraft away from an airfield designated 'Foxes Two'. As they came into land on the airfield they believed was no longer in German hands, they began to take fire. Raymond's new CO was hit and his tail was blown off. He crashed and was killed instantly. Raymond took hits too and knew he was going to have to make a wheels-up landing. On approach he heard a scream across the radio: 'Bax! Bax! Get your tank off!' He struggled with the release handle and got it off just in time to land in a vineyard, narrowly avoiding an olive tree. In a cloud of red volcanic dust he clambered from the cockpit and fell to the floor with an injured knee and the unnerving sound of gunfire close by. He looked up to see a US army medic. 'You a Hun?' the medic asked, about to swipe Raymond with an entrenching tool. They were within feet of a fully marked RAF Spitfire.

A Jeep then approached driven by a tearful US colonel. He explained that the Americans had panicked and fired on the British aircraft thinking they were enemy. CO Andy Anderson had been killed, Raymond shot down and five other aircraft damaged. Raymond was mentioned in dispatches during the campaign.

Near the end of 1943 Raymond fell ill with jaundice and went back to the UK. There then followed six months of 'on rest' flying as an instructor at Montford Bridge, Shropshire.

On evening during this posting he was invited to a nearby American OTU. He pushed open the swing doors to the officers' mess and saw 'this beautiful, beautiful girl standing at the bar in a green evening dress who I asked to dance'. It was Second Lieutenant Sylvia Kathryn Johnson, an American nurse at the 64th Field Hospital at Oulton Park. Over the coming months they had many idyllic outings in his MG sports car.

Five weeks after D-Day Raymond was posted to mainland Europe with his CO, Max Sutherland DFC: 'The most dangerous man I ever met, but I almost adored him.' Sutherland made Bax the leader of 'A' flight of 602 City of Glasgow Squadron, flying his favourite variant of the Spitfire, the clipped wing mark XVI. The squadron supported operations along the Rhine at Eindhoven and Arnhem. Patrolling in the clouds they were buzzed by a German jet, the radical ME262. The weather hampered attempts to support ground troops at Arnhem. The squadron was 'knocked about a bit' and got withdrawn to RAF Coltishall to re-equip and learn dive bombing. In response to Hitler's V2 attacks, 602 strafed roads, cut railway lines, destroyed bridges, and generally harried the German forces. In a later interview Baxter said of flying over a V2 site during a launch with his wingman firing at the missile, 'I dread to think what would have happened if he'd hit the thing!'

In March 1945, Sutherland hit upon a daring idea. He addressed his four most senior officers:

'Outside The Hague is the former HQ building of Shell-Mex. It is now the centre of operations for both V1 and V2 attacks. I have worked out that the width of the building is equal to five Spitfires flying in close formation wing-tip to wing-tip. I reckon we can take it out'. He looked Raymond in the eye: 'What do you reckon, Bax?'

'It might be a bit dodgy, Boss,' replied Baxter.

Although flak was a daily experience for them, attacking this target would put them at the mercy of up to two hundred batteries of well manned guns.

'Yeah, I know,' replied Sutherland, 'but we'll get 453 [squadron] to lay on a diversion, and then we'll go in low and flat.'

453 were an Australian unit in the same fighter wing. The attack was agreed, and after the first intended date was aborted due to poor visibility, they launched again. Passing the Dutch coast at 8,000 feet 453 branched off and Sutherland transmitted the code word 'buster' (full throttle) and the order 'close up'. They dived to one hundred feet and with the target three hundred yards ahead they let loose with two 20mm cannons, 0.5-inch machine guns, one 500lb bomb and two 250lb delayed timer bombs. As they passed the target Raymond barely avoided a cockerel weathervane on a church spire and Sutherland had his tail shot up badly. The five planes dispersed, but Sutherland took some more flak while attempting to look back at the target. He had damage to his starboard elevator and Bax escorted him back to their base in Belgium. Sutherland was awarded a bar to his DFC while Raymond Baxter and the others were mentioned in dispatches. Years later aviation artist Michael Turner recreated Raymond's cockerel moment in a painting. A Dutchman who as a boy was in the caretaker's quarters of the Shell-Mex building at the time saw the painting and wrote to Raymond to thank him and the other pilots for risking their lives. He said, 'I heard you coming, and I looked into your eyes.'

602 flew in support of the liberation of the Channel Islands and flew their last operation two days before VE Day. Eleven days later 602 was disbanded. Within a month Raymond was posted to Cairo where he flew Mustangs and later DC3 Dakotas. His time with Spitfires was over.

It wasn't long before Raymond and Sylvia started to miss each other. Sylvia was staying at the US Army leave centre near Mulhouse in France. Raymond pulled out all the stops and hitched two flights, only to arrive and find Sylvia was travelling with friends in Switzerland. But he managed to get a message to her: 'Please come back and marry me.'

On the afternoon of 20 September 1945 Raymond and Sylvia were married in the leave centre's cinema. Raymond was in his best blues, Sylvia's dress was made from parachute silk, their ring was made by a German prisoner of war silversmith from a smelted English half crown, an American silver dollar and a German mark. The CO lent them his staff car for a honeymoon in the French countryside.

In March 1946 Raymond walked into the studios of Armed Forces Broadcasting in Cairo and asked if they had any jobs. He was tested reading the NAAFI News and three weeks later he was posted to HQ MEDME Welfare (Middle East & Mediterranean). Raymond was the only officer at the station so he immediately became CO, but the place was run by an army NCO who had been the chief announcer at Radio Luxembourg before the war. Raymond made guest appearances on Egyptian State Radio reading the news on their English service. With the help of the British consul in Boston, Sylvia arrived in Egypt to join Raymond in Cairo. Later in 1946 Raymond Baxter was demobbed from the RAF and he and Sylvia returned to the UK.

Wanting to pursue a career in broadcasting, particularly with the BBC, Raymond took a job with the British Forces Network in Hamburg over the winter of 1946/47. There he witnessed people dying in the streets from hunger and exposure. He also crossed paths with Cliff Michelmore and aspiring actors who would become big names: Bryan Forbes, Roger Moore and Nigel Davenport; as well as technical staff who would progress to the BBC. Raymond and Sylvia spent the late 1940s in Germany, witnessing and reporting on the Berlin Airlift.

Raymond Baxter joined the BBC in 1950. He provided radio commentary on the funerals of King George VI in 1952 and Winston Churchill in 1965, the former given from high up near the ceiling of Westminster Abbey. He reported at the coronation of Queen Elizabeth II in 1953 from Trafalgar Square, and the wedding of Princess Margaret. He broadcast for the funeral of Lord Mountbatten of Burma, becoming emotional at the sight of Mountbatten's horse being led with stirrups reversed carrying his empty riding boots. Raymond provided commentary on many of the State visits of the Queen in the early years of her reign. He covered the D-Day anniversary broadcasts in 1974, 1984 and 1994. He was especially touched when he watched the march-past on Pegasus Bridge led by wheelchair-bound Major John Howard who had commanded the heroic glider assault on the bridge fifty years before. He was pushed along by the pilot who had flown his glider.

In 1953 Raymond took part in the London to Christchurch air race. He received an invitation to join as a co-pilot, unpaid, but also as the official BBC commentator. The steward of the flight was one John Profumo, parliamentary secretary to the Minister of Transport and Aviation. By all accounts he executed his duties in exemplary fashion.

From 1950 almost every year until 1986 Raymond attended the Farnborough Air Show as a BBC correspondent, during which he flew with the Red Arrows and piloted a Hawker Harrier. He also reported on the maiden flight of the Concorde and was a great friend of its chief test pilot Brian Trubshaw. He was the first reporter to broadcast from an aeroplane, ocean liner and underwater.

He was the BBC's motoring correspondent from 1950 to 1966, reporting on Formula One races, the Le Mans 24-hour race and the Monte Carlo Rally. His first BBC commentary for a motor sport event was from Goodwood in Sussex for the British Automobile Racing Club Easter meeting of 1950. Raymond requested a list of drivers beforehand and contacted as many as he could. After that he was the BBC's principal motor racing commentator for the next 23 years. His first television commentary was from Silverstone in 1953. His first live broadcast was in 1955 from Monte Carlo. Sylvia kept 'lap charts' of the race and they witnessed Stirling Moss racing at his height of his powers.

'Bax' was immortalised in an edition of the *Victor* Comic in December 1963, covering his life as a war hero, a motor sport competitor and all round 'boys' own' hero.

He was parodied in 1958 by Peter Ustinov in *Grand Prix du Roc* as 'Roland Thraxter' who would shout, 'Mind my tea, it's on the edge of the table!' Baxter and Ustinov met at the famous but now long gone Steering Wheel Club in Mayfair (on my 14th birthday my father took me to the Steering Wheel Club. I knew it was special but I didn't know how special until too late! Today I pass its door in Shepherd's Market feeling hugely nostalgic). He made a cameo appearance in the 1966 John Frankenheimer movie *Grand Prix* as a trackside commentator/interviewer, although in his autobiography *Tales of my Time* he says he disliked Frankenheimer's arrogant brashness, felt he hit the European racing scene like a bull in a china shop, and missed the opportunity to make the definitive motor racing movie. Raymond also appeared in the *The Fast Lady* and *The Green Helmet*.

Raymond commentated in an episode of *Hancock's Half Hour* when Tony Hancock entered the Monte Carlo Rally, and in the game 'Mornington Crescent' on BBC Radio 4 show *I'm Sorry, I Haven't a Clue*. He appeared on *Michael Bentine's Potty Time* and with Spike Milligan on his *Q* series: 'Funeral by rocket – bury your loved ones in space', as well as numerous other TV appearances.

Sylvia died in 1996, and he gave up commentating at the Royal British Legion's annual Festival of Remembrance at the Albert Hall: 'I could not trust myself to cope with what was always an emotionally demanding experience.'

Raymond was good friends with Stirling Moss. He was at Goodwood in 1962 when Moss inexplicably charged off the circuit, crashing heavily and sustaining severe brain injuries: 'I visited him at the Atkinson-Morley Hospital and he could scarcely complete a sentence. I secretly wept for the loss of one of the most articulate of men. Yet within three years nobody noticed anything had happened. He had willed his mind to re-orientate to bypass the damage. He was and still is the epitome of courage, skill and determination, as well as being an extremely nice man. Sir Stirling Moss is truly a legend in his own lifetime.'

He was also good friends with twice Formula One world champion and pilot Graham Hill. When Hill was killed on 25 November 1975 it hit Raymond badly.

Connection to motor racing through the 1950s and 1960s provided a direct link to danger and death. Not only did Raymond feel the tragedy of the loss of drivers in accidents he might not have witnessed, he did bear witness to what is probably motorsport's most horrific single incident: the Le Mans tragedy of 1955 when a Mercedes cartwheeled from the track into the main stand killing seventy-two and injuring more than one hundred people.

From 1949 Raymond Baxter competed in numerous Monte Carlo (the Montes), Alpine, Tulip and RAC Rallies, winning his first trophy in Hamburg. His first international event was the Lisbon Rally of 1950 at the invitation of a businessman, 'Goff' Imhof. Raymond was his co-driver and went on to compete with him at Monte Carlo and the Tulip Rallies in Holland.

An association with one-off car maker RW gave Raymond the chance to race in single-seat cars. He progressed to drive at the Montes, first in Austins and Fords, then in works Jaguars and the Aston Martin DB3. In 1960 he raced in the same team as Paddy Hopkirk, and in 1964 in the legendary BMC Mini Cooper team. He competed in the Monte Carlo Rally twelve times, six of them as a member of the BMC works team.

From 1967 to 1968 he was briefly Director of Motoring Publicity for the British Motor Corporation. Following BMC's takeover by Leyland Motors, it was decided to dispense with Raymond's services, and he returned to work full-time for the BBC.

He presented the science series *Eye on Research* from 1959 to 1962 which covered topics from radio astronomy to cryogenics to viruses.

Baxter is best known amongst a certain generation for being the first presenter of the BBC science and technology programme *Tomorrow's World*, which he did from 1965 to 1977. The show regularly reached an audience of ten million viewers. During a live broadcast in 1967, Raymond interviewed South African surgeon Christiaan Barnard by telephone within hours of completing the world's first heart transplant. On the programme he was also the first passenger to cross the English Channel by Hovercraft.

Raymond left *Tomorrow's World* in 1977 after disagreements with its new editor Michael Blakstad over Concorde. Blakstad devoted an entire show to the aircraft's failings at a crucial time for its future, which created a conflict of interest for Raymond.

Raymond presented the first 'Raymond Baxter Award for Science Communication' in July 2000. He was surprised to find that he was the first recipient. He was made an honorary freeman of the City of London in 1978 and awarded the OBE in 2003. He was vice-president of the Royal National Lifeboat Institution from 1979.

In 1998 he was the subject of *This Is Your Life*. He was recording a voiceover at a Soho recording studio when Stirling Moss's voice came over the headphones. He emerged from the soundproof booth to be confronted by Aspel, Moss and a cameraman.

Raymond was a founder member of the Association of the Dunkirk Little Ships. He owned one of the small vessels that evacuated British troops from the beaches. He was also honorary chairman of the Royal Aeronautical Society from 1991.

Avuncular and charming commentator, brave Spitfire pilot and racing driver, Raymond Baxter will long be remembered for inspiring a generation of fans of *Tomorrow's World*. He died peacefully aged 84.

Chapter 14

Staff Sergeant Ken Miles (1918-66)

Tank Recovery Specialist in the Second World War

Sports Car Driver & Engineer

True winner of Le Mans 1966

Kenneth Henry Miles was born on 1 November 1918 in Sutton Coldfield to parents Eric and Clarice. Ken was a maverick from the start. At the age of 11 he had his first taste of the perils of the internal combustion engine when he rode a 350cc trials bike in the dark and crashed it. He struck a lamp post after losing control on an unfinished road repair which resulted in the first of many broken noses.

He also developed a fascination with guns at an early age. Once he used the neighbour's apple crop for target practice, much to the neighbour's disapproval. Ken, thinking himself unfairly treated, sought revenge. He climbed up a tree and onto his neighbour's roof when he was entertaining church dignitaries and dropped a dozen live frogs down the chimney.

On another occasion he fell off the roof of his grandparents' house and crashed through a glass roof into the middle of a knitting party. By good fortune he was unharmed.

A childhood interest was taking things apart to see how they worked; Meccano was his favourite toy.

At a young age he met Mollie, who he vowed he would one day marry. Of Ken's education, Mollie later commented: 'As a scholar he was a dead loss, and even as an adult it was difficult for him to decipher his own handwriting. He is, however, an avid reader and can carry on discussions on the most varied of subjects.'

At 15 he tried to run away from home and go to the United States, but he failed and he settled into an apprenticeship at Wolseley Motors.

Wolseley was founded as the 'Wolseley Sheep Shearing Company' but, their product being seasonal, in the 1890s they diversified into car production and car production soon became their primary business. Young Ken went from sweeping the floors to assembly and fabrication.

Wolseley sent him to technical school, and one day he would become a highly regarded race car engineer, development driver and driver.

With Mollie he acquired an Austin Seven car. She painted it British racing green while he tweaked its performance. He was too young to race or to obtain a driving licence, but that did not stop him driving it.

As a teenager, Ken made friends with a lad called John Beazley, another Wolseley apprentice. Ken's grandparents' house was a few doors down from the Beazleys. In the war, during an air raid, incendiary bombs set Ken's house alight and John and others in the neighbourhood helped put the fire out. John and Ken would still be friends after the war.

At 16 he bought a Velocette motorcycle. He had a driving licence by now, but he soon lost it for speeding.

In November 1939 Ken found himself in a Territorial Army camp and posted to an anti-aircraft unit in an armament-producing area. It was an exciting posting and lasted for a year. Next he was posted to a driver training regiment in Blackpool, where he taught soldiers how to drive army vehicles. Ken recounted that the worst candidates were former London taxi drivers who were convinced that nobody could teach them anything. During his time in Blackpool his nose was broken again in a brawl.

Mollie and Ken married in 1942 and he was sent to join the Royal Corps of Electrical and Mechanical Engineers (REME) and promoted to staff sergeant. To complete this move Ken had to undergo a technical training course in the south of England. He emerged with the highest marks. He was then posted to a tank unit on the east coast.

Between 1942 and 1944 Ken was moved around the UK several times, breaking his nose twice more, before landing in Normandy, according to Mollie's recollection, on D-Day 'plus two'. In August 1943 he had a letter published in *Motorsport* magazine in which he declared his intention to fit a supercharged engine into a competition car after the war.

On D-Day the armoured vehicles of the REME beach recovery sections landed immediately after the assault, to be closely followed by crawler tractors and wheeled recovery vehicles. They worked extremely hard, under shellfire, having to avoid mines, explosive charges secured to underwater obstacles, and visits from enemy aircraft night and day. 'Drowned' vehicle parks were established near the beaches for the repair of waterlogged vehicles and guns.

Armoured brigade workshops were given high priority. By the afternoon of D+1 three complete workshops were functioning and by D+3 seventy-five per cent of the workshops had landed. Ken would have been heavily involved in all of this, up to elbows in grease, oil and sand.

Between D+2 and D+11 669 vehicles were brought into the workshops, 509 were repaired and returned to units, 130 were classified as beyond local repair, and the remainder written off.

After Normandy Ken saw service in France, Holland, Belgium, and Germany. His specialism was tank reconnaissance and recovery, the latter often being a horrific job as many of the vehicles he recovered still had the wounded or dead occupants inside, or parts of them. The Germans referred to the mainstay Allied Sherman tanks as 'Ronsons', in reference to how easily they 'lit up' (caught fire).

Ken's unit was the first to pass though Bergen-Belsen concentration camp, where he would have witnessed more horrors.

After the German surrender, he was stationed close to the Baltic coast where, until he was demobilised in January 1946, he spent time organising motorcycle races and sailing yachts.

He returned home to Wolseley and moved with Mollie into a new house in Moseley, Birmingham. As Mollie says, 'He bought a Frazer-Nash car to race when I wasn't looking,' and fitted a supercharged Mercury V8 engine, as he had promised. In his first race at Silverstone in April 1949 he came second.

By 1951 John Beazley had become the general manager of Gough Industries in southern California, who were the local MG distributor. Beazley was looking for a manager for his service department and chose Ken. Ken moved there in December 1951 with Mollie and now with their son, Peter.

In April 1952 Ken drove his first race in a Gough Industries MG-TD and his driving ability became apparent. In 1953 he won fourteen straight victories in the Sports Car Club of America racing series in an MG-based special of his own design and construction.

But his wayward nature came to the fore in May 1955 when he was fired from Gough as a result of a disagreement with the company controller Phil Gough.

With his great skill and talent, both as a driver and mechanical engineer, Ken Miles was a key member of the Shelby/Cobra race team in the early 1960s: 'I am a mechanic. That has been the direction of my entire vocational life. Driving is a hobby, a relaxation for me, like golfing is to others. I should like to drive a Formula One machine, not for the grand prize, but just to see what it is like. I should think it would be jolly good fun!'

Ken had a reputation for courtesy on the track and was sometimes called the 'Stirling Moss of the West Coast'. With a pronounced Brummie accent and a sardonic sense of humour, he was affectionately known by his American racing crew as 'Teddy Teabag' (for his tea drinking) or 'Side-bite' (as he talked out of the side of his mouth).

After leaving Gough, Ken worked in the motor industry for several other companies, and then in 1960, continuing to race sports cars with great success, he established his own sports car business in North Hollywood. He and Mollie became US citizens in 1959. But by 1962 Ken's shop was forced to close due to unpaid taxes; he had ploughed too much money into racing.

Between 1958 and 1963 Ken won 38 of 44 races he entered, also driving part-time for Sunbeam distributor 'Rootes', and the likes of Carroll Shelby were becoming aware of his driving and engineering ability. He was picked up by Carroll Shelby to test and race the Cobra – a partnership that was immortalised on screen in the 2019 movie *Ford vs Ferrari* (released in the UK as *Le Mans '66*). He became the chief test driver of Shelby American in 1963 and competition manager. He also had a hand in developing the Sunbeam Tiger for the Rootes Group.

Ken raced Ferraris from time to time, including a 375 Plus Spider in 1955, which he took to third behind Ernie McAfee and Phil Hill, later Formula One and Le Mans drivers. Phil Hill would join Ken in Shelby's squad alongside Parnelli Jones, Dan Gurney, Bob Bondurant, Chris Amon, Bruce McLaren and Roy Salvadori among others.

Ken's racing record continued to astonish, helping Shelby to the 1964 USRRC (United States Road Racing Championship) constructors' title, taking first with Lloyd Ruby in the 1965 Daytona Continental race, second in the Sebring Twelve-hour Race with Bruce McLaren in a Ford GT40, and winning at the Laguna Seca circuit in a Cobra.

He and Ruby won the 1966 Daytona 24 Hour race for Ford and Shelby American in a GT40, with GT40s sweeping all of the podium places. The Ruby/Miles pairing won again at Sebring in March that year in a Ford GT40 roadster.

But his greatest triumph came at Le Mans. In 1966, MkII GT40s were dominating the Le Mans 24 Hours race, occupying the top four positions until the Jerry Grant/Dan Gurney car retired with a blown head gasket.

Shelby was ordered by Henry Ford II to orchestrate a formation finish to trigger a dead heat, with Denny Hulme/Ken Miles in the lead ahead of Bruce McLaren/Chris Amon in third. Ken slowed down, realising that in the event of a dead heat the qualifying times might be used and McLaren would have been declared the winner. Jaded by Ford's orders and hostility towards him over many years that included excluding him from the 1965 team (Henry Ford II and Leo Beebe of Ford just did not like him), he resigned himself to taking second place and McLaren was the winner. The win actually came down to McLaren having travelled further, as he had started about eighteen yards further back on the grid than Ken.

In 1966 the Ford J-car was intended to be the successor to the all-conquering Ford GT40 MkII and, despite reliability problems, showed potential in the springtime pre-Le Mans trials. After the death of Walt Hansgen in a Ford J-car while testing at Le Mans in April, the decision was made to shelve the J-car and focus on the proven MkII, and little development was done for the rest of the 1966 World Sports Car Championship season. Finally, in August, Shelby American resumed testing and development work with Ken serving as primary test driver. The J-car featured a 'bread van shaped' rear section that experimented with new aerodynamic theories, as well as a revolutionary but untested honeycomb panel design that was supposed to both lighten and stiffen the car.

After almost a day of testing at Riverside International Raceway in the brutally hot Southern California desert summer, Ken approached the end of the track's mile-long, downhill back straight at a top speed of over 200 mph when the car suddenly looped, flipped, crashed into the ground and caught fire. It broke into pieces and ejected Ken, killing him instantly.

As a result, the aerodynamics of the J-car were greatly modified to correct the rear-end lift generated at race speeds. This would later save the life of driver Mario Andretti.

In 2001 Ken Miles was inducted into the US Motorsports Hall of Fame. He is probably the greatest racing driver most people have never heard of. The following description by his biographer Art Evans perhaps sums up why he did not have the success which from his incredible talent one might have expected:

'I am fully aware that all who came into contact with Ken Miles didn't necessarily find it smooth sailing. Even though he lacked much formal education, he was highly intelligent and didn't suffer fools. One of his failings, I think, in personal relationships, was that he would often let the fool know about his foolishness.'

Chapter 15

Carroll Hall Shelby (1923-2012)

USAAF in the Second World War

Racing driver, Le Mans winner, engineer & sports car manufacturer

Carroll Shelby was born on 11 January 1923 to Warren Hall Shelby, a rural mail carrier, and his wife Eloise (née Lawrence) in Leesburg, Texas. Shelby suffered from heart valve leakage at 7 and experienced problems with this throughout his later life. In his biography he recalled that if he didn't rest during the afternoons he would get very tired. He grew out of what he described as a 'heart murmur' in his teens, but it would come back to plague him at the zenith of his racing career.

From a young age Shelby had a fascination with speed, leading to an interest in cars and aeroplanes. His father was an avid car enthusiast, buying an Overland open top touring car in late 1927. The Overland was his pride and joy and he cherished it. The first time Shelby went for a ride in it he sat on his father's lap and was allowed to grip the steering wheel; from that moment it appears Shelby was hooked. Later in 1928 his father replaced the touring car with an Overland Whippet that was fitted with wire wheels which particularly fascinated Shelby. He described its 'new car smell being the sweetest perfume in the world.'

He moved to Dallas, Texas, at 7 with his family as his father had got a job in the city post office. At 10 he would ride his bicycle to dirt tracks nearby to watch races on the oval circuits sometimes called 'bull rings'. Eager for a car of his own, at 15 he was driving and taking care of his father's Ford, and he acquired a 1934 Dodge that needed some repairs to make it his own. Watching the great drivers of the day doing battle on the oval dirt tracks inspired him to become a racing car driver one day. Shelby recalled four drivers in particular: Gene Frederick, Herschel Buchanan, Oscar Coleman and Tex West.

At high school in Dallas, Shelby was interested in flying and golf. Golf was affordable as a hobby but flying clearly wasn't, so he found a tradesman's way into it, becoming involved in aircraft mechanics.

In 1939 as war broke out in Europe Shelby met Jeanne Fields. They would marry in December 1943.

In 1940, aged 17, Shelby left high school with a view to becoming a race car mechanic, to find a way into the sport and raise money to do so. He would have liked to become a commercial pilot, but his parents couldn't afford to send him to college that was a necessity for the training.

While still 17 he bought an Excelsior motorbike and began making deliveries for a local drug store. One day on a poor road surface he skidded, hit a kerb, and landed with the bike on top of him, bruising himself badly. He abandoned the bike there and then, quit the drug store job, and as soon as he turned 18 headed to the army recruiting office.

As America wasn't yet in the war, he and two friends were offered to join the US infantry and go to the Philippines, but Shelby refused stating he wanted to join the US Army Air Corps. His friends joined up while he decided not to, but as he was walking away Sergeant Smith, the recruiting officer, called after him, 'Son, you really want to join the Air Corps?'

'Yes, I sure do,' said Shelby.

'Leave me your number and I'll call you if we get any Air Corps openings.'

Sergeant Smith called him the next day, telling him he would have to go to New York State. Shelby again turned Smith down saying, 'New York's still a long way from Texas.'

Two days later Smith called Shelby yet again: 'You better get ready to sign, you can go to Randolph Field here in Texas if you want to join the Air Corps.'

He passed his physical assessment in Dallas and then went to Randolph Field. Up to this point Shelby's flying experience amounted to holding the controls of an aircraft in exchange for sweeping out some hangers, a couple of trips in a biplane as an 11-year-old, and a flight arranged by his father in a Ford Trimotor.

He commenced training with seventy-five other recruits billeted in a leaking tent, doing drill, physical exercise and chores such as mopping hangers. They were fed well and Shelby claims he grew six inches during his basic training, although he stayed skinny. He and the other recruits expected glamourous jobs once they had finished their training, but he found himself shovelling chicken manure around Randolph Field's flower beds. He spent three months doing this before deciding to deliberately commit a discipline offence to get out of work. He and a friend dug a hole for their sergeant's tractor to tip over into; it worked and they got five days in 'the brig'.

On release, Private Shelby became a fireman ready on the flight line and spent three months driving a fire truck. As the shooting war was about to begin for the USA he joined a selection process for air crew training. As he was about ten pounds underweight he stuffed himself with bananas and milk and qualified in November 1941.

He then moved to Lackland Army Air Force base to learn radio communications, navigation, engineering and mathematics.

This completed, Shelby was moved to Cuero, Texas, where he learned to fly a Fairchild PT-19. Shelby was hospitalised for two weeks with pneumonia, but his instructor worked extra time with him to coach him up to speed. Although Shelby had much praise for this man, he was critical of the overall approach to training in that era. He felt that the service was more interested in how many they could fail instead of how many they could pass. He also felt that the high failure rate was due to the poor standard of the instructors.

Shelby said, 'You're always nervous the first time you go up in that grabber by yourself with nobody there to tell you what to do if something goes wrong. The first time I went up solo I overshot three or four landings in about ten or fifteen minutes.'

He moved on to intermediate training, with pursuit or twin-engine aircraft, at Sherman, Texas, and at Ellington Field near Houston in September 1942 was promoted to flight sergeant. In December 1942 he was commissioned as a second lieutenant through what was called the 'air students' scheme' for those without a college education.

Shelby never wanted to rise to high rank. He preferred to have fun and keep his responsibilities to a minimum. Once he took Jeanne and his future mother-in-law for a pleasure flight over Texas, and sometimes he would also fly over Jeanne's home and drop a letter to her in an old flying boot.

Shelby finished his twin-engine training at Ellington Field and then went on to fly trainee navigators and bombardiers from San Angelo in Texas in the twin engine Beechcraft. Later he flew larger bombers, the B-18, B-25, B-26, and finally the B-29 from Denver, Colorado. He was such a good instructor that he was never deployed overseas in combat.

He also spent time as a test pilot, experiencing many of the dangers of combat flying such as malfunctions, pilot error, wheels-up landings, and parachuting out of aircraft.

Once he was flying a Beechcraft with two trainee crewmen on board when an electrical fire broke out. He told them to bail out but one was reluctant to do so. Shelby screamed at them over the intercom to get out and one pushed the other out. In the commotion Shelby had failed to fasten both leg straps of his parachute. He jumped out and when the parachute opened he was upside down. He hit the ground with no idea where he was and ended up with a thirty-five-mile walk back to base in the dark. His progress, despite an injured hip, was hastened by the sound of howling coyotes.

On another occasion he was flying a Beechcraft AT-11 when because of an air bubble in the fuel system both engines stopped. There was no chance of restarting. It was daylight so he planned a wheels-up landing on some farmland. As they hit the ground and the aircraft began to slide the bomb bay doors were torn off, after which clouds of dust were thrown into the aircraft. Shelby, despite being dazed from striking his nose on the control column, managed to leave the aircraft safely with the trainees.

Shelby and Jeanne married on 18 December 1943 and Jeanne had their first child in September 1944. At the time, Shelby was flying B-29s from Denver, Colorado.

After the war Shelby went into the trucking business with a life-long friend called Bailey Goodwin. Hauling ready-mixed concrete using dump trucks they made good money and expanded the business. In 1947 Shelby branched out into hauling timber too.

A second child, a son, was born in November 1946, and then another in October 1947.

The post-war house building boom had helped the business succeed, but Shelby knew it would not last forever and he sold it.

In 1948 and 1949 he worked as a 'roughneck' in the oil business, then he became a chicken farmer. His first brood netted him a good profit but the second caught Newcastle's Disease and he went bankrupt.

It was January 1952 before he got his first racing break with friend Ed Wilkins who asked him to enter a drag race in a home-built car. Shelby blew the competition away and was soon invited by Wilkins to enter a sports car race in an MG TC. In May 1952 in Norman, Oklahoma, Shelby won with a good margin. Then he took on a field of Jaguar XK120s in a modest MG TC and beat them.

In 1953 he raced exclusively for Roy Cherryhomes in Cad–Allard cars. He had a successful season.

He was described as 'the genial Texan with his trademark distinctive striped, bib-style racing overalls'. The overalls gave him the appearance of a sort of swashbuckling Casey Jones. In truth he had gone in a hurry to a race meeting from what remained of his chicken farm in his agricultural overalls and because he was late he didn't have time to change. By chance he found them cooler than his normal driving outfits. They attracted much attention, so much so that he decided to stick with them as a kind of hallmark of who Carroll Shelby was.

In 1954, Kleenex heir Jim Kimberly, one of the great racing philanthropists of the time, had donated a prize for a race between American and Argentinian drivers. Shelby entered the Buenos Aires 1,000 km sports car race in the Cad-Allard, co-driving with airline pilot Dale Duncan, who was a useful contact when it came to air freighting the car to Argentina. They finished 10th despite a carburettor fire during a pit stop which had to be extinguished by the simple expedient of Duncan urinating on the engine. More significantly, Aston Martin driver Peter Collins introduced Shelby to his team manager, John Wyer, who had been impressed with the Texan's handling of the wild Allard. Shelby now had an entry into Aston Martin. This would lead to a place in their works team and a memorable victory at Le Mans five years later.

Wyer offered him a drive in an Aston Martin DBR3 at the Sebring endurance race. Shelby accepted. With his co-driver he was making good progress during the first three hours of the race but when the rear axle failed his race was over.

Wyer had invited Shelby to the UK, which led in May 1954 to him driving a DBR3 at Aintree in US colours, coming second in a strong field. This performance won him a place in the factory team in the 1954 Le Mans 24 hour race. He and Paul Frère were doing well but had to retire with a mechanical failure.

Shelby made a fifth outing in the DBR3 in Monza, Italy, where he finished fifth winning $2,000. He then raced for the final time with Aston at Silverstone, coming third.

In late summer 1954 he returned to America to race again for Roy Cherryhomes in a C-Type Jaguar.

However, in August 1954 Donald Healey of Austin Healey in England invited Shelby to help set seventy new Class D speed and endurance records at the Bonneville Salt Flats in Utah. About 110 miles into one race, near Oaxaca, Shelby struck a large rock, flipping his Austin Healey four times. He was badly cut, his elbows were shattered and several other bones were broken. Native Americans found him and offered him alcoholic drinks to ease the pain while waiting for help. In March 1955 he was back on the track, with his hand taped to the steering wheel and his elbows in a custom-made fibreglass cast.

Shelby teamed up with Phil Hill in a 3.0 litre Monza Ferrari for the Sebring race of March 1954, coming second, his arm still in a cast.

During the 1955 season Shelby drove for a wealthy businessman called Tony Paravano, entering a race in August at the disused Bremerton airfield in Seattle driving a 4.9 Ferrari 375. Two of his competitors were Phil Hill and Ken Miles. Shelby won, with Hill coming second and Ken Miles, with whom he would go on to form a close friendship and partnership, coming third.

In the same season Shelby raced for Paravano against Stirling Moss and Mike Hawthorn at the Ards Circuit at the TT race in Northern Ireland at which three drivers were killed.

To start the 1956 season Shelby drove a Maserati until a specially built Ferrari 4.9 arrived for him that had originally been prepared for Fangio.

In Shelby's biography he recalls winning eighteen of the twenty races he entered, but he was proudest of coming second to Fangio in Cuba in October. Because of this performance he was crowned driver of the year by *Sports Illustrated*.

In 1957 Shelby travelled to Italy to drive for Ferrari. When the question of how much he would be paid came up, Ferrari said he was still a new driver and the privilege of racing for Ferrari should be enough. Shelby walked out and went to Maserati.

The season was successful for Shelby, although he did not finish at the Sebring Endurance race, a contract with Maserati for a Formula One drive fell through, and he had a nasty crash in September at the Californian Riverside Raceway and suffered facial injuries.

In November, again at the Riverside Raceway, Shelby, racing a Maserati V-8, spun out on the first lap and then was forced to wait for twenty seconds before being allowed to rejoin the race, ending up at the back of the field. He then went on to demonstrate a driving masterclass passing everybody, including Dan Gurney and Walt Hansgen, going on to win the 100-mile-long race. When interviewed he said, 'After making a darn fool of myself on turn seven I reckon I just got mad!'

'Carroll Shelby Sports Cars', dealing in European sports cars, was founded with oil businessman John Hall in Dallas in 1957.

In 1958, with his marriage deteriorating, Shelby went back to race in Europe, having reached a deal with John Wyer at Aston Martin. Part of his aim was to make contacts in the sports car producing community. This was also the year he developed his concept of a light-weight, well-proportioned, high-performance sports car. His car would be a rival to the Corvette, the only real American-built sports car, and a rival to those that came over from Europe. He conceived of an Austin Healey type car with a V-8 engine producing around 300 bhp. There was one problem: no-one he spoke to was interested in supporting the idea; most thought it had no merit.

Shelby spent most of 1958 in Europe driving for Aston Martin in either a DBR1 or a DBR3, partnered much of the time with British driver Roy Salvadori. He dabbled briefly with Formula One, driving for a private team called Scuderia Centro Sud. He drove a dated and uncompetitive 250F Maserati but did well, finishing sixth. He also drove Formula One in an Aston Martin DBR4 in the 1959 season. These were front-engine cars when the fashion and technology were turning to rear or mid-engine cars, so they were obsolete even before they raced for the first time.

But Aston Martin were to have great fortune at the 1959 twenty-four hours of Le Mans. The team entered three DBR1/300s with a stellar line up of six drivers: Moss/Fairman, Trintignant/Frère and Shelby/Salvadori. Ferrari entered four cars and were the favourites with Dan Gurney and Phil Hill on their team. Also driving were Jim Clark, Jo Bonnier, Bruce McLaren and Graham Hill. Ferrari led for most of the arduous race but faded mechanically in the last few hours. Shelby and Salvadori finished first, Trintignant/Frère second, while Ferrari took the next four places. Moss had retired with engine problems. Shelby describes the race as the greatest of his life.

Then in September Salvadori and Shelby clinched the World Sports Car Championship for Aston Martin at Goodwood.

In 1960 Shelby moved from Texas to California. California was the heart of the growing 'hot rod' movement and he thought it would be a good place to find engineers to help him produce a low volume sports car.

Shelby began to experience chest pains in early 1960. A friend who had previously had a heart attack offered him some nitro-glycerine tablets to try, and sure enough they took the pain away. His doctor incorrectly diagnosed the problem as 'referred pain' from a neck muscle. Eventually in California he was diagnosed with angina pectoralis, a hereditary condition. He was advised to retire from racing but he continued to race through the 1960 season as he was determined to win the American sports car championship.

Having to take more and more nitro-glycerine tablets to get through each day without pain, his last race was in December, the Third Annual Los Angeles Times-Mirror Grand Prix for sports cars. He drove a Type 61 Birdcage Maserati and finished fifth, winning the USAC driving championship for 1960. Then, aged 37, he quit race driving for good.

His next venture was to set up the Shelby 'School of High-Performance Driving' along with sports car engineer and driver Pete Brock, fresh from the Corvette project with General Motors. The school was run from the Riverside Raceway. Shelby was also managing his own Goodyear Racing Tyre distributorship.

Shelby's ambition to manufacture a high-performance American sports car was now more set in his mind than ever. He heard in 1961 that the British AC Car company could not get Bristol engines anymore as the Bristol Aeroplane Company had folded. So he brokered a deal that saw AC switch to the new 4.7 litre Ford V8. Dave Evans at Ford America gave Shelby some engines to 'play around with them, see what you come up with and let me know'. Shelby did so, and the AC Cobra was born. Ford backed him and the Shelby Cobras were approved as GT cars by 1963.

Shelby's workshop was established in Venice, California, in March 1962 with a wealth of enthusiastic engineering and fabrication talent.

In January 1963 what was now 'Shelby American' signed Ken Miles to drive a Cobra and he was placed second (behind his teammate) at Riverside Raceway, both of them beating the previously dominant Corvette Stingrays. Miles was so confident in the car that he pitted for a drink of water and then re-lapped the Stingrays to finish.

By June Shelby American had completed its first 125 Cobras. To sell his first few cars Shelby would have them repainted every day to make it appear he had lots of them!

Although they were a partnership, Ford declined to finance any Cobra entries for Le Mans, so Shelby struck a deal with AC Cars and American driver Ed Hugus. The top Shelby AC Cobra finished seventh.

In October 1963 Shelby American began to work on what would become the Daytona Coupe, aiming to achieve 200 mph on the Mulsanne straight at Le Mans. Pete Brock, now an essential engineer at the Venice facility and still teaching at the racing school, was tasked with designing it. In February 1964 Shelby American completed the first Daytona Coupe.

Shelby American won the domestic US GT car championship in 1964, but it would be 1965 before the Shelby Daytona Coupes won their FIA GT car championship class, snatching this prestigious title from their Ferrari opposition.

Meanwhile, Ford introduced its new Mustang sports saloon (in American English, sedan) at the New York World's Fair in April 1964. Ford vice-president Lee Iacocca promised the car would be 'a sports car suitable for street use or competition'. In reality the Mustang was not a great sports car, and Iacocca hired Shelby to improve it. Thus the truly legendary Shelby Mustang GT350 was created, with upgraded intake and exhaust manifolds, carburettor, rear axle and brakes installed in place of the standard Ford parts at Shelby American's shop in California.

At the 1964 24 Hours of Le Mans the Shelby American Daytona finished first in the GT classes and fourth overall, beaten only by the prototype Ferraris, the 275P and the 330P. Ford's new prototype, the legendary GT40, fared poorly in this race; none of the three cars entered finished. At the end of the 1964 season Ford handed control of the GT40 program to Shelby American.

Under Shelby's management the GT40 driven by Lloyd Ruby and Ken Miles won the first race of the 1965 season at Daytona. Then Miles and Bruce McLaren finished first in the prototype class and second overall at the next race at Sebring. Apart from that, the GT40 program was a disappointment, once again failing to finish at Le Mans that year.

Shelby American worked with Ford to re-engineer the GT40 for the 1966 season, replacing the 289 cubic inch (4.7 litre) engine with Ford's 427 (7.0 litre) engine. The Mk II GT40 achieved great success, with Shelby American wins at Daytona, Sebring and Le Mans earning Ford the International Manufacturer's Championship in 1966. Shelby American cars finished first (Miles & Ruby) and second (Gurney & Jerry Grant) at Daytona, first at Sebring (Miles & Ruby), and first (McLaren & Chris Amon) and second (Miles & Denny Hulme) at Le Mans. Gurney and Grant would have finished second at Sebring except their car broke down on the last lap and Gurney pushed it across the finish line, automatically disqualifying them. I have explained elsewhere that Ken Miles was the true winner of Le Mans in 1966.

In March 1967 the final 427 Cobra was built and in September 1967 planning began for the Cobra's successor. It was christened 'The Lone Star' and a prototype was built in England by JW Automotive. In August 1968 the last new 427 Cobra Roadster was sold (until 1995) and then in October 1968 the only Lone Star produced was put up for sale at $15,000.

During the 1966 season Shelby and Ford were developing the J-car, a more advanced version of the GT40. But on 17 August 1966 Ken Miles was killed at the wheel of a J-car while high-speed testing at Riverside Raceway. Shelby was very upset by the death of a close friend and collaborator in achieving his dreams.

With work on the GT40 program and production of the GT350 beginning to ramp up, Shelby American ran out of space at their shop in Venice, and in 1965 moved to an aircraft hangar at Los Angeles International Airport.

After the 1967 season the FIA changed the rules for prototypes, and the 7.0 litre engine used in the Mk II and Mk IV GT40s became redundant. Shelby American withdrew from the World Sportscar Championship transferring control back to Ford's original management choice, John Wyer's Automotive Engineering. JWA GT40s won the 1968 and 1969 races at Le Mans, giving the GT40 program an unprecedented four consecutive wins.

For 1967 Shelby decided to install the Ford 7.0 litre engine in the Mustang creating the GT500. Revised front and rear facias distinguished the 1967 Shelby Mustangs from the common Fords they were based on.

Shelby Mustangs sold well, and after 1968 Ford took control of the Shelby Mustang, moving production in-house.

After the 1969 season Carroll Shelby withdrew from competition and in January 1970 he closed the automotive business. Thereafter Shelby American was defunct.

Now Carroll Shelby began to diversify. In 1967 he had advertised a deodorant called 'Carroll Shelby's Pit-Stop' sold with the tagline 'A Real Man's Deodorant'. Then, having held a chilli cooking competition, he began marketing his own chilli mix. Then in 1974 he left the USA for South Africa. There he sold 'Carroll Shelby's Original Texas Brand Chilli Preparation'. His little brown packets promised to 'shake the meanness out of the most ordinary, leather-mouthed chilli-head that was ever born.' In July 1986 he sold the company to Kraft.

In August 1976 the first annual convention of the 'Shelby Automobile Club of America' was held in Oakland, California, attended by Shelby, some of his former drivers, and 600 self-confessed 'Shelby-philes'.

Cars remained deeply ingrained in Shelby's life. In October 1982 Shelby agreed a contract with Chrysler to create performance cars based on Dodge products. Shelby recalled: 'I should never have got back into it, but I couldn't turn Iacocca down. He was in trouble, and he'd always been good to me.' It didn't take long. In November the prototype 'Dodge Shelby Chargers' were completed and displayed.

In 1987 Shelby and Chrysler began work on the Dodge Viper RT/10. The supercar was ready in time for the 1989 Detroit Motor Show.

In June 1990 Shelby underwent a heart transplant operation, the new organ coming from a 38-year-old gambler who had a stroke at a Las Vegas gaming table. Less than a year after his transplant, Carroll Shelby paced the 1999 Indianapolis 500 in a Dodge Viper. Before the race, and in breach of the track rules, he and former *Motor Trend* editor-in-chief took the Viper out for a spin. Van Tune later recalled: 'Blasting down the straight between turns 2 and 3, Carroll legged out the car in fifth gear. I couldn't see the speedometer but it felt like 120-125 mph. Suddenly, he grabs his chest and slumps over in the seat. Oh my god, Shelby's had a heart attack, I thought. After the three seconds it took to have my life flash before me (and to grab the steering wheel) Shelby sat up, roaring with laughter. "Ha! I got you, Tune!" Carroll jested. He laughed and laughed.'

Post-race doctors said his heart was as strong as anyone's. Later that year he established the Shelby Heart Fund.

At Lime Rock Shelby raced a 1965 Shelby 'R' GT350 for the first time. Now 69, he lapped just half a second off the record set in the same car in 1965. The following month he was inducted into the Automotive Hall of Fame.

In 1993 he told the Cobra replica manufacturers they could keep building cars if they donated $1,000 per car to his charity. Twelve agreed.

In 1995 Shelby began production of a series of 427 Cobra Roadsters. Over half the purchase price of these cars was donated to the Shelby Heart Fund. Eventually the Shelby Heart Fund became the Shelby Children's Foundation.

In September 1999 Shelby's original Cobra prototype was named by *Motor Trend* the most significant car of the last fifty years: 'Were it not for this car, there would be no Shelby Cobras of their designations of 260, 289 or 427, no Daytona Coupes… Were it not for this car, there would've been no Shelby Mustangs. Likewise, were it not for this car, what would be the chances of the Shelby–Chrysler connection ever happening? If not, count out the likelihood of there ever being a Dodge Viper.'

In 2003, as the Ford Shelby Cobra Concept was revealed at the Detroit Motor Show, Shelby said: 'This is it. This is my last hurrah. I'm going to end my car-building days where I started them: with Ford.'

In February 2011 Shelby was honoured with the Keith Crain/Automotive News Lifetime Achievement Award, and in May he was recognised by the World Children's Transplant Fund for his donations to organ transplantation over the years.

Carroll Shelby, flying instructor and test pilot in the war, winner of the 1959 Le Mans 24 Hours, inventor of the AC Cobra, died aged 89 on 10 May 2012 in Dallas, Texas. He had been married seven times and had three children, and his automotive legacy was almost as great as that of Ferrari.

Chapter 16

Murray Walker (1923–2021)

Tank commander in the Second World War

British Motorsport's greatest commentator

Graeme Murray Walker was born in Hall Green, Birmingham, on 10 October 1923 to a family of Scottish descent. His father, Graham, had been a despatch rider in the First World War for the Royal Engineers Signals Service and then a works rider for the Norton Motorcycle company. He competed in the Isle of Man TT. Murray's mother, Elsie, was the daughter of Harry Spratt, who owned a prosperous drapery and clothing shop in Leighton Buzzard. Murray was their only child. When he was 2 the family moved to Wolverhampton as his father had been appointed competition manager for Sunbeam Motorcycles. Another move followed three years later as Graham became competition director for Rudge-Whitworth.

Up to the age of 8 Murray was educated by a governess, after which he attended several prep schools. He then went to Highgate School in North London where he gained a distinction in divinity (like Bertie Wooster!). He also learned to play the bugle and became a company sergeant major in the school corps.

Aged 15 in August 1939 Murray and his father attended the International Six Days Motorcycle Trial being held in Austria. His father had been invited by the War Office to advise the Army team. The local German organiser was adamant that war was not likely as Germany and Russia had signed a non-aggression pact. But on day five of the trial, with the British team in the lead, a War Office telegram instructed everyone to 'return home, war imminent'.

For Murray the trip had been amazing: a long car journey to Salzburg with spectacular Alpine scenery and quaint Austrian hotels, and then a dash home just in time to escape being trapped in enemy territory. Three years later Murray would take part in the conflict.

When war broke out, Highgate School was evacuated to Westward Ho! in Devon.

His call to service came in October 1942, taking the train from Waterloo to Dorset to report for duty as Private 14406224 at the 30ᵗʰ Primary Training Wing, Bovington. Bovington is and was the home of the Royal Armoured Corps, with gunnery ranges at nearby Lulworth, and training facilities for all things 'tank', so driving, maintenance, wireless operation and busy workshops. The association with people from all social and economic backgrounds was by Murray's own admission a great life education.

Murray observed that training as a basic soldier with its harsh discipline was all about creating a mindset of unquestioningly following orders in battle; he thrived and respected it. Completing this first phase, he moved to the 58ᵗʰ Training Regiment of the Royal Armoured Corps and became 'trooper' from private. He learnt all disciplines of being a tank crewman: driving, gunnery, wireless and command instruction. He could ride a motor bike, but before learning to drive a tank, troopers had to learn to drive a fifteen-ton truck. As a result of the prevailing times, by his own admission and following demobilisation from the army in 1947, Murray never took an official driving test. Physical and soldiering training continued alongside the specialised armoured training, where Murray found his nemesis in Morse code. Before completing his training, he went down with pneumonia, and following later attendance at a War Office Selection Board he was selected for officer training.

Before entry into the Royal Military Academy at Sandhurst, Murray had to attend Pre-Officer Cadet Training at Blackdown Camp in Surrey, where he learnt the continued lessons of listening out, not making assumptions and staying sharp. A year on from his initial entry into the army as an enlisted man Murray made it to Sandhurst; it was October 1943 and he became part of 115 Troop, Officer Cadet Training Unit.

Twenty-three trainees commenced training with 115 Troop with eighteen graduating as second lieutenants six months later. There was the constant pressure of potential failure, and an ever-present emphasis for all officer candidates on determination, leadership and initiative. Murray developed his respect for the 'poor bloody infantry' with a week-long infantry battle exercise in North Wales and an ascent of Snowdon. The exercise included everything from digging trenches, to living off the land, to section attacks on invulnerable positions. Carrying their heavy infantry kit as well as additional equipment, such as mortars, they made the 3,500 foot ascent of Snowdon. It did reinforce his sense of operating in tanks, where you didn't have to walk and always had a roof over your head.

Murray passed out from Sandhurst on 8 April 1944 with American General Dwight Eisenhower as his reviewing officer. In his biography Murray said, 'Even 57 years on I can still feel the excitement and pride of that parade, arms swinging, and boots resounding to the beat of the drum and the music of stirring military marches.'

Murray set sail from Harwich, landing in Normandy using the famous 'Mulberry Harbour' at Arromanches, and posted to the battle-hardened Royal Scots Greys as a tank commander. It was an intimidating posting for the new officer as the Greys had seen fierce action in the Western Desert of North Africa with General Montgomery and acquitted themselves well. The Greys had not only fought in the advance to Tripoli, they had fought in Italy, Normandy and through France to Belgium and to Holland where Murray joined them in the town of Nederweert.

On reporting to his new commanding officer Murray had a typically amusing encounter that seemed to fit with so much of his life. Major Sir Anthony Bonham said to Murray, 'Welcome to the regiment, George, we are glad to have you with us.'

Murray, slightly embarrassed, replied, 'Sir, the G is for Graeme, actually. But my friends call me by my second name, Murray.'

Bonham looked disappointed. 'Oh, I thought Murray-Walker was a hyphenated double-barrelled name.' Murray observed that he thought his new boss was disappointed that, being a cavalry regiment, a young officer with such a monied sounding, gentrified, double-barrelled name fitted more with their officers' profile.

Murray's first 'live war' experiences were sentry duty overnight standing in the turret of his Sherman tank, then soon after using his vehicle to deliver ammunition supplies to the American 101st Airborne troops engaged in clearing dug-in German resistance. During the fighting they tried to take rest as safely as they could, and in seeking comfort at times Murray came across the divides that had occurred in Dutch communities as a result of the war. He encountered a woman who had had her head shaved for being an alleged collaborator.

War held many experiences for tenacious young men, including a challenge where Murray (driving a jeep) was goaded to try to catch up with a B17 bomber taking off from an airfield. Not only did he drive furiously enough to catch it up, but he smashed the top of the jeep's windscreen against the bomber's tail.

In February 1945 the Greys were in action on the borders of Germany at the Reichswald Forest and the banks of the River Rhine. Working with the infantry the tanks were heavily involved in operations to displace and force back fierce German resistance. This involved danger from snipers, negotiating ditches, encountering blown-up bridges and overcoming the mentality of an enemy who were fighting for their homeland to the death.

Murray had seen many horrors since his arrival, and then came a very emotional interlude. His unit was resting, refuelling, rearming and allowing others to leapfrog ahead as they did so, and Murray was sitting on the edge of his turret with his legs dangling. He watched as four men ambled towards him in army uniform with one resembling his father. As they closed in, he realised it was his father. Graham Walker, adorned in battledress, smoking his pipe, and at the time the editor of *Motor Cycling* magazine, had himself been accredited as a war correspondent with the express intention of finding his son. This was a special moment in Murray's war, and it is easy to understand why, after the training he'd been through and the horrors he had seen.

Murray witnessed the distressing results of the Allied mass bombing raids. Passing through what was left of the town of Udem, Murray recalled, 'The thousand bomber raid that destroyed it must have left it like Dante's Inferno. The roads were blocked by rubble, bodies were strewn around, houses were still ablaze, and there was a nauseating smell. Bemused cattle were wandering around, there were people shouting and guns firing. I had the constant worry of the Germans firing an 88mm anti-tank gun or letting you have it with a Panzerfaust. V-1 rockets were soaring over us aimed at Antwerp. We advanced through stubborn and dogged resistance of Panzers and elite paratroopers and marines.' By 24 February 1945 the Reichswald was cleared.

Murray witnessed the sound and sight of a 3,300-gun artillery barrage on the German positions on the other side of the Rhine and watched the paratroop and glider operations following it. He saw the horrific sight of a light reconnaissance tank falling from the back of a 'Hamilcar' glider. The Tetrarch tank emerged from the back of a glider hundreds of feet in the air, all the crew on board, and plunged to the ground. The airborne assault that he witnessed was a total success, and on 25 March Murray and his tank crossed the Rhine.

Bitter fighting continued, and it is hard to imagine the placid and gentle Murray we all knew from British television standing across the body of a dying elite German Marine. Murray had his pistol in hand ready to dispatch the marine in case he was faking it. Like most veterans, Murray 'liberated' a few souvenirs, some Zeiss binoculars from an 88mm gunner, who had tried to destroy his tank, and eventually a P38 Walther pistol.

At this time the politics of the inevitable German surrender came to the fore. Who would take Berlin, the American/UK forces or the Russians? The Germans were trapped in a closing vice, but the German soldiers did not want to surrender to the Russians for fear of the retribution they would receive. There were the concerns over Russian dominance, so a decision was made for the Western Allied forces to get to the Baltic coast first.

In what must have been one of the most bizarre sights, Murray's brigade was advancing at speed towards the coast heading east while German soldiers were racing west at the rate of five thousand troops per hour to avoid the Russians. They were passing each other on the same road. Both sides ignored each other, each with very different goals. For Murray it was a surreal and exhilarating advance, including an eighty-mile dash in one day, no mean feat for a slow-moving tank with a top speed of barely 30 mph on a road heavy with retreating and advancing traffic. That was 2 May, and on 8 May Germany surrendered. Murray picked up one more souvenir. His words: 'A German officer's knife with a swastika and an engraving on the blade of "God is with us." Funny that, I thought he was with us,' he reflected.

In October 1946 he became technical adjutant to the British Army of the Rhine Royal Armoured Corps Technical Training Centre at Belsen. It was the Belsen of infamy, but by the time Murray was there it had been turned into 'Caen Barracks' with all vestiges of the camp removed. It had been transformed into British barracks with no hint of its previous purpose.

Murray's war had come full circle. He began as a humble private at the centre of all things tank in Bovington, England, and finished in the German equivalent of Bovington as the captain adjutant. While there Murray engaged in motorcycle racing before being demobilised from the army in May 1947 and returning to Britain.

After demobilisation he began a career in advertising, working for Dunlop before becoming accounts director for the Masius advertising agency, whose clients included British Rail, Vauxhall and Mars Confectionery. Murray denies having invented the slogan 'a Mars a day helps you work, rest and play' but he did create 'Opal fruits, made to make your mouth water.'

In the motorsports season of 1948 he competed in motorcycle events, and soon discovered his ambition exceeded his ability. Competing against the likes of seven-time world motorcycle champion and one-time Formula One champion John Surtees, Murray quickly recognised his limitations. But an invitation to commentate for the Shelsley Walsh Hill Climb of 1948 changed the course of his career.

So impressive was his commentary at Shelsley Walsh that Murray was given a recorded audition for the BBC in 1949 at the Easter Monday Goodwood Race, and on 14 May he was positioned at Stowe Corner at Silverstone with another commentator called Max Robertson for the British Grand Prix.

This was a radio commentary, but his opportunity for television came later that year at the Knatts Valley hill climb.

After that he received regular broadcasting work.

With his father he covered the Isle of Man TT every year until his father's death in 1962. Murray said on the death of his father: 'The motorcycling world had lost a colossus, and we shall not see his like again.' Among his father's many achievements was setting up the motorcycle section at the Beaulieu Motor Museum. Murray's parents had moved there in 1954.

Motorcycles were Murray's first love. In 1962 he became the BBC's chief motorcycle racing commentator, and in 1963 he co-authored *The Art of Motorcycle Racing* with Mike Hailwood.

Murray dabbled in Formula One commentary in the 1970s before taking it up full time in 1978. Through the next three decades he covered motocross, motorcycle racing, Formula One, British Touring Cars, the Macau Motorcycle Grand Prix, the Bathurst 1000 Australian touring car race, Formula Three, Formula Ford and truck racing.

From the Monaco Grand Prix in 1980 through to the Canadian Grand Prix of 1993 Murray struck up an unexpectedly successful commentating double act with wild playboy Formula One champion of 1976 James Hunt. Initially the pair did not get on – Hunt once wrestled the microphone out of Murray's hand only to be grabbed by the lapels by Murray and threatened with a fist. But after that they became good friends.

After Hunt's death Murray had other commentating partners, including Jackie Stewart, Martin Brundle, Jonathan Palmer and Alan Jones.

Murray was renowned for occasionally getting his facts mixed up, and also sometimes saying how well a driver was doing and then for it all to go wrong. These became known as 'Murrayisms'. When at the 2000 German Grand Prix he confused Ferrari drivers Michael Schumacher and Rubens Barrichello he decided it was time to retire.

He then wrote an autobiography, *Unless I'm very Much Mistaken*, which I would highly recommend.

Through the 2000s he remained active and took part in many challenges. He competed as a navigator in the Targa Tasmania and Targa New Zealand tarmac rally races; he became Honda Formula One team ambassador for a season; he attended the Isle of Man TT centenary in 2007 to help make a documentary; he co-authored the *Murray Walker Scrapbook*. He also wrote several Grand Prix yearbooks, as well as profiles of his greatest heroes.

In 2006, probably following years of exposure to loud engines and guns, Murray lost his hearing in both ears. He then became chief ambassador to David Ormerod Hearing Centres.

Murray Walker chose to stand while commentating. He said it allowed him to speak louder, with his lungs better inflated and his shoulders back. He prepared himself for every piece of commentary work by meticulously researching facts and statistics on every driver and racetrack, updating and rewriting them for the following event. He had an encyclopaedic knowledge of Grand Prix racing. Drivers and team members would almost always agree to be interviewed by him.

Walker received the OBE in 1996 for services to broadcasting and to motorsport, and in 2009 he was voted 'the greatest sports commentator of all time' in a poll conducted by British sports fans. Captain Murray Walker gave much more than motorsport commentary to modern society as part of a great generation and their commitment to service.

Murray passed away, while I was writing this book, on 13 March 2021. This book is dedicated to his memory.

Chapter 17

Second Lieutenant David Purley GM (1945-85)

1st Battalion The Parachute Regiment

Formula One & Formula Two Racing Driver

David Charles Purley was born in Bognor Regis, West Sussex, on 26 January 1945. His mother, Joyce, was Welsh. His father, Charles, changed his name from Puxley to Purley. Charles, who had no formal education, was the founder of LEC refrigeration. He had begun his business empire buying and selling crates of fish and delivering them by bicycle. LEC stands for 'Longford Engineering Company'.

David was educated at Seaford College, from which he was expelled for persistent lateness (he claimed his alarm clock failed to go off twice). After that he went to Dartington School, the innovative school in Devon founded by Leonard Elmhirst.

After school David worked as LEC's company pilot for nine months, but he left after a row with his father.

He then joined a demolition company as a 'top man' working on tall buildings in London. This was a dangerous job, especially in winter when the buildings were icy.

When the company folded, David signed up for a three-year stint with the Coldstream Guards. On arriving home, his mother was not pleased.

After brief service as an enlisted man, he accepted a commission and completed his officer training at Sandhurst. He then joined First Battalion, The Parachute Regiment, as a second lieutenant and was posted to Aden.

Purley was like a cat with nine lives. His first was used up parachute training when his chute became entangled with that of an instructor. The two men descended at speed below what was left of the instructor's canopy. They plummeted for around a minute and a half to 'a heavy landing', but they survived.

In Aden, Purley may have used up another life or two as British forces faced regular mortar, grenade and machine gun attacks. Purley survived several near misses. Purley survived a direct attack with a rocket propelled grenade. It impacted into a wall behind him with Purley then retrieving some of the fallen masonry as a souvenir, returning it to the family home.

He said, 'Under those circumstances, you've got to have a certain lack of imagination. It's no good being highly sensitive when you're firing or being fired on. There were times when I've never been so frightened in my life. What happened out there, what I did and what I saw, has never worried me, but it made me hard. I won't be pushed around by anyone.'

It was during his final year in the army, 1969, that he became drawn to motorsport, inspired by his friend Derek Bell, also Sussex-born.

After army service he shared an AC Cobra with his cousin Derek Ridler. David admitted he was a 'pretty hairy driver' and wrote the car off at Brands Hatch. But motorsport had got into his blood and the following year he was out in a Chevron B8 sports car.

LEC would help support David Purley's racing career, and in 1969 he set up his own Formula Three team with two mechanics, fully entering the racing world of single seaters in 1970. He raced a Brabham car under the LEC Refrigeration banner, winning his first race a few weeks later, beating James Hunt at the Grand Prix des Frontières at Chimay in Belgium. Purley said: 'Chimay was a very fast, dangerous, circuit which used to get my adrenalin going. Throughout my racing career, I always drove faster when I was slightly nervous such as at Chimay, the Nürburgring or at Rouen. It gave an edge to my driving. For this reason, I was never particularly quick in practice unless we'd had problems and I had to screw myself up to get a time in the last few minutes of a session.'

At Oulton Park on Good Friday 1972 in his Formula Two debut he claimed pole position. But his race lasted only 200 yards before his throttle cable broke; it was won by Niki Lauda in heavy rain.

For the 1973 season, his team purchased a March 73B race car and rented another for competition in two British Formula Atlantic Championships (a UK domestic championship that was a stepping stone to Formula One for many drivers and constructors). Purley finished runner up in one of the Atlantic championships.

He qualified for Formula One later in 1973, and in the Monaco Grand Prix he was the quickest March driver until he crashed. He was the second quickest March driver behind James Hunt at the British Grand Prix at Silverstone, then came Zandvoort.

At the Dutch Grand Prix, fellow British driver Roger Williamson crashed badly and was trapped in his overturned and burning car. Purley abandoned his own race and attempted to save Williamson. As he arrived at the scene he heard Williamson crying for help. Purley's efforts to right the car and extinguish the flames were in vain. He received no help from nearby track marshals or emergency workers. Other passing drivers also failed to come to his aid. Williamson died. Zandvoort already had a reputation as a dangerous circuit since the death of Piers Courage in 1970 and nothing had changed.

Purley was recognised for his courageous actions by being awarded the George Medal.

Purley's attempt to rescue Williamson was televised live. 'To be honest,' Purley was to say later, 'I think it ruined my motor racing career because afterwards I was never the racing driver but always the chap who won the George Medal. I looked on it as a great honour but, remember, I'd been in the army and half my brother officers and the men I'd been serving with had been decorated for gallantry. I'd daily rubbed shoulders with men who had received similar awards.'

Three years later Purley would tell *Autosport* magazine that his actions were the natural reactions of a man who had spent time in the armed forces: 'What happened was purely a reflex action. In the service, if one saw a burning tank or something, one tried to help the people inside. With Roger's accident it was exactly the same. It was a case of a man needing help.'

In 1973 two British racing drivers were awarded the George Medal. The other was Mike Hailwood, who had gone to the aid of Clay Reggazoni's burning car in South Africa.

A week later he raced at the Nürburgring, which would become synonymous with another fiery and near fatal crash in 1976, that of Niki Lauda. Purley had to face the pressure of publicity. When he arrived at the circuit the officials were at pains to show him the safety arrangements and the firefighting equipment.

During practice for the race, Purley was extremely slow – too slow to qualify. But, unknown to him, all the other drivers had signed a petition asking the organisers to allow him to start regardless of his time. He brought his March 731 home in fifteenth place.

Purley raced once more in Formula One in 1973, at Monza where he finished ninth.

In 1974 he competed in Formula Two and came fifth in the series. He raced against Patrick Depaillier, Tom Pryce, Jacques Lafitte and Patrick Tambay and he achieved three second place finishes.

For 1975 there had been an intention to move into Formula One, but a deal fell through, so Purley formed a team to compete in Formula 5000. The Chevron B30 car he competed in ran with a Cosworth developed V6 engine which had reliability issues. The truth was, Purley was not one to run repeated development laps to hone a car's potential. In the season he achieved two wins and came fifth in the series.

The 1976 season showed his ability with six wins out of thirteen rounds and taking the 'Shellsport' British F5000 title. This time development of the car had been financed by LEC and managed by Purley's friend, five times Le Mans winner Derek Bell.

1977 saw a full-scale assault on Formula One with the enthusiastic financial support of LEC and David's father, although in Formula One terms the LEC team was run on a shoestring. But the car was always well presented and Purley was driving well even if he was at the back of the grid. The early Grand Prix outside Europe were given a miss, the team joining the F1 circus for the Spanish race, for which Purley failed to qualify. He was also so far off the pace in Monaco that the team withdrew. In Belgium he began to move up the grid, qualifying in twentieth place and finishing thirteenth. In Sweden he was nineteenth on the grid and was classified fourteenth at the end. In the French GP he started in twenty-first but crashed on lap four. Although he was not giving Lotus and Ferrari sleepless nights, he was qualifying ahead of a dozen other drivers. In a wet and dry race at Zolder in Belgium, Purley actually led for half a lap before pitting for slick tyres; he later reckoned he might have won had it kept raining. Not realising that Purley had led the race, Niki Lauda, who believed he had been held by him, stormed up to Purley's pit at the end of the race to complain about the 'rabbits' in the race. Purley told him to get lost in a forthright way, but at the next race the LEC car appeared with a rabbit painted on the side of the cockpit.

At the British Grand Prix at Silverstone a small electrical fire broke out in Purley's car that a marshal promptly doused with an extinguisher. By the time the car was back in the pits there was only fifty-five minutes to prepare for the second pre-qualifying run. Team manager Mike Earle said later, 'Had we had a larger budget he could have switched to our second car which was ninety-five percent complete in our workshop. I ordered the team to change the engine but that would have eaten into the second session and David reckoned he needed the full session to set his time. What no one knew was that some extinguisher foam in the throttle slides jammed them open and as he approached Becketts [a corner on the circuit] Dave went straight on and into the barrier.'

It has been calculated that Purley stopped from 110 mph in just over two feet. The impact stopped his heart but prompt action by a doctor revived him. When Mike Earle arrived on the scene Purley began to argue with his team manager about the cause of the accident. The doctor encouraged Mike to keep on arguing to keep Purley conscious while he was cut out of the car. He was not expected to survive the twenty-mile ambulance drive to Northampton General Hospital, but he did, although he was in constant pain for the next six months. He suffered twenty-nine fractures in total and his heart stopped six times during treatment.

When Purley climbed into his second LEC Formula One prepared car in August 1979 at Goodwood his left leg was one and a half inches shorter than his right. Had he come close to his previous best time it would have been an incredible achievement. As it was, within thirty-six laps he had bettered his previous best. As soon as he saw the pit board he braked and called the session to a halt. For Purley it was another challenge successfully overcome.

Purley then raced the LEC car and a Shadow DN10 four times in the UK Aurora Championship, picking up fourth place at Snetterton. For Mike Earle, long time team manager, it was the most satisfying result of their long association. He said, 'David came back into the pits and the crowd broke into applause. He called for me to push him round the back and help him out. He was in agony but didn't want to show it.'

David Purley never raced a single seater again after 1979.

Not happy with his left leg being shorter than the other, he eventually tracked down a Belgian surgeon who was prepared to undertake an operation to break his left leg, stretch it by a millimetre a day, and then graft in bone. There were two snags, it would be extremely painful, and the operation had never been performed on an adult before. If it failed, it would leave him a permanent invalid. This was a step into the unknown.

But months later he was walking again, and not only walking but taking part in Enduro motorcycle races.

In 1981 he bought a Pitts Special biplane and became a familiar sight over the south coast. Initially he hoped to become part of the British aerobatics team, but although he was a competent pilot, capable of doing all the stunts seen at air displays and flying competitions, his routines were not tight and disciplined. Typically, Purley said, 'I can't be bothered about that envelope of air you have to stay in to stand a chance in competition.' Ironically he maintained that aerobatics was less dangerous than motor racing, despite surviving two crash landings. When he crashed into the sea off Bognor Regis on 2 July 1985 motor racing lost one of its most popular drivers. He had recently entered his second marriage and he and his wife Gail had a daughter.

A memorial was erected in 2017 close to the site of the former LEC factory in Bognor Regis. It is inscribed with the words:

Gone now your eager smile
high held head and soldier's stride
etched were skies by your elegant style
and this earth enriched by your pride

David Purley was never quite an 'ace'. He was perhaps born at the wrong time to be successful with his approach. It is said that his attitude, talent, and flamboyance belonged to the fifties or early sixties. He did, however, embody so many of the qualities which are representative of motor racing at its best, and whenever great characters of the sport are remembered, one of them should be David Purley GM.

Chapter 18

Mike Hailwood (1940-1981)

Motorcycle racing world champion

Formula One driver

Le Mans 3rd place 1969

Stanley Michael Bailey Hailwood MBE GM is the only subject of this book without a connection to military service, but like Dave Purley he was awarded a George Medal for his bravery.

Mike was born on 2 April 1940 at Langsmeade House, Great Milton, Oxfordshire. He had an older sister called Christine. His father Stanley, 'Stan', raced in the pre-war era and became a millionaire from founding the Kings Group of motorcycle dealerships.

Mike's parents separated when the children were quite young and he was sent to boarding school at Purton Stoke, Kintbury. He then went on to Pangbourne Nautical College, where he wore a naval-type uniform, this being the closest he came to military service.

His parents separated when the children were quite young.

Mike learned to ride at age 7 on a minibike in the fifty-two acres of fields around his home, Highmoor Hall near Henley-on-Thames. Highmoor Hall is a ten-bedroom mansion built during the reign of Charles II. Stan had removed the kick-start from the 100cc Royal Enfield so he had to learn to bump-start it. He also had a 100cc mini child's car and an ex-RAF Link flight simulator.

Mike saw his first race at age 10, when he went with his father to the Isle of Man TT races.

Mike hated Pangbourne College and left when he was 16. He would not miss the cold showers, iron discipline and at least one beating that he would remember forever. His main interests while there were music and boxing. He boxed for the college on 14 occasions with 13 wins and one split decision.

On Sundays after regimental parade he would go home and ride, and he soon progressed to a 197cc James Commando trials bike. His father could see that Mike had talent as he watched him ride around a makeshift trials course. Unbeknown to Stan, he was also driving his stepmother's Jaguar XK120.

After leaving school, Mike worked for a short time in the family business. His father then sent him to work at Triumph motorcycles. While there he developed his desire to go racing, and Stan set about making his racing career a reality.

He first raced on 22 April 1957 at Oulton Park when he was barely 17. His next race, five days later at Castle Coombe, saw him finish fourth in the 125cc class and fifth place in the 250s, and he started to get noticed. Then in June he won his first race at Blandford Camp in Dorset in the 125cc class, followed in July by another win, in the 250cc class at Snetterton. This caught the eye of John Surtees, who at that time had won one motorcycling world title and would go to win six more. Surtees lent Mike a bike to race in South Africa over the winter. This was like giving him a whole extra season in the year. He did this several more times in future years.

In spring 1958 he was placed second on a 250cc at Brands Hatch and then a few days later won two first places at Crystal Palace. That year he won ACU Stars at 125cc, 250cc and 350cc classes earning him the Pinhard Prize, awarded annually to the motorcyclist under 21 who had achieved the most during the year. He teamed up with Dan Shorey to win the Thruxton 500 endurance race and finished well in four classes of Isle of Man TT races with one podium. In the 1957 season Hailwood won 5 races; by the end of 1958 he had won 58.

The 1959 and 1960 seasons saw him continue to ride consistently well in all classes, achieving his first GP win on a 125cc Ducati at the 1959 Ulster Grand Prix (sometimes he rode Nortons and NSUs, but mostly he rode Ducatis). He finished third overall in 1959 in the 125cc championship.

1960 didn't see as many great results. His highest finishes were two third places in the 500cc GP class at the Isle of Man and the GP of nations at Monza.

In 1961 Mike signed with an up-and-coming Japanese factory named Honda, and in June he became the first man in the history of the Isle of Man TT to win three races in one week. He nearly won a fourth but his 350 AJS broke down with a failed gudgeon pin. Riding a four-stroke, four-cylinder, 250cc Honda, he won the 1961 250cc world championship.

In 1962 Mike signed with MV Agusta and went on to become the first rider to win four consecutive 500cc world championships. He also started to race cars with their factory team. From 1963 to 1965 he drove a Lotus 24 and 25 and a Lola Mark 4 in non-championship Formula One races.

In February 1964 during preparations for the US motorcycle Grand Prix, Mike set a new one-hour speed record on the MV 500cc, recording an average speed of 144.8 mph on the oval-shaped, banked speed-bowl at the Daytona circuit.

By 1967 Mike had won twelve times on the mountain course of the Isle of Man TT, including what many consider to be the most dramatic Isle of Man race of all time: the 1967 Senior TT against his great rival Giacomo Agostini. In that race he set a lap record of 108.77 mph on a Honda RC181 (a 500cc GP machine) that stood for the next eight years.

He won the 250cc and 350cc championships for Honda in 1966 and 1967 and then said he intended to re-sign for Honda provided the 1968 machinery was to his satisfaction. But then he stated to *Motorcycle Mechanics* magazine that even without suitable machinery from Honda he would not go elsewhere, and that he would in any case retire at the end of the 1968 season.

At the end of 1967 he went to South Africa where he started a building business with a former motorcycle Grand Prix rider, Frank Perris. They completed their first house in October 1967 and then sold another to South African ex-racer Jim Redman.

Honda pulled out of Grand Prix racing in 1968 but paid Mike £50,000 not to ride for another team, in expectation of keeping him as their rider when they returned to competition. Mike continued to ride Hondas in 1968 and 1969 in selected race meetings without world championship status.

In 1968 he won twenty races despite breaking his collar bone at a hill climb event in Switzerland in July. Mike appeared in selected UK events in 1968, appearing in the post-TT race at Mallory Park on a Honda, and in 1969 he participated in the Mallory Park Race of the Year. By this time he was tired of bike racing and wanted to race cars.

He started by being placed third in the 1969 Le Mans 24-Hour in France as co-driver of a Ford GT40 with David Hobbs. Also in 1969 he drove in the World Sports Car Championship, and the Guards Formula 5000 championship in which he finished third.

What is less well known about Mike Hailwood is that he had a stellar career on four wheels as well as two. He first raced in the British Grand Prix on

20 July 1963, and in 1964 he achieved two podium finishes and scored 29 championship points. He came close to victory at the 1971 Italian Grand Prix where he and three other drivers finished in the first four positions split over just two-tenths of a second; Mike finished fourth. Had he concentrated on cars instead of motorbikes he could well have been a title contender.

But in 1970 he was back bike racing, on a Rocket 3 750cc at the Daytona 200 race in Florida, part of a BSA/Triumph team. While at the head of the field the machine overheated and he was forced to retire. Mike again rode for BSA at the 1971 Daytona race, qualifying on the front row. Again he was leading the race, when this time an engine valve broke.

1971 onwards saw Mike fully engaged in four-wheel endeavours, signing for the 1971 season with John Surtees' F5000 team driving the Surtees TS8 car, coming second in the Rothmans national championship. Towards the end of that season Surtees gave him a drive in his Formula One car at the Italian Grand Prix; he led several times during the race and eventually came fourth. This led to racing in Formula One and Formula Two with Surtees in 1972 (their cars sponsored by Matchbox Toys). He did better in Formula Two than in Formula One – he won the European Formula Two championship in fact. Mike had a great working relationship with John Surtees; though Surtees was a Formula One car world champion, they both had a foundation in motorcycle racing. Mike stayed with the Surtees team for the 1973 season.

At the 1973 South African Grand Prix, local driver Dave Charlton lost control of his Lotus at Crowthorne Bend and was hit by Mike's Surtees TS10. Clay Regazzoni and Jacky Ickx arrived where the collision had occurred and ploughed into Mike's stationary car. Interlocked, two of the cars burst into flames with Regazzoni trapped inside his. The monocoque body of Regazzoni's car had been split by the impact. Mike got out of his car and rushed over to Regazzoni's car. Seeing that the stricken Swiss driver was unconscious he undid his safety harness. Mike himself caught fire and had to abandon the burning car to put out his own flames by rolling on the grass. Meanwhile the marshals put out the fire, or they seemed to have done. However, the two cars caught fire again, with Regazzoni still in his car. Mike returned to the inferno and finally managed to haul Regazzoni out of his car.

Pauline, Mike's wife, was watching the race from the pits: 'Mike came into the pits stony faced. We were staying with an old bike racing pal called Paddy Driver. Mike just took me to the bike we were riding and we went back to Paddy's. He said nothing about the fire or saving Regazzoni's life.

It was only when I read about it in the papers the next day that I found out what he'd done.'

Mike received the George Medal , which is awarded for gallantry 'not in the face of the enemy'.

In 1974 Mike signed as a works driver for the Yardley-sponsored McLaren M23 and impressed the paddock immensely, sometimes outpacing team leader, teammate and 1972 world champion Emerson Fittipaldi.

But in the second last lap of the 1974 German Grand Prix at the Nürburgring Mike crashed head-on into the Armco. His ankle was shattered so badly that he could never drive competitively again. Surtees' view was that Mike was only just about to hit his peak, not because his driving had improved but also because he had a greater understanding of the sport.

Mike, Pauline and their two children then upped sticks for New Zealand where he established a boat business.

Four years later, on 3 June 1978, after an 11-year absence from mainstream motorcycling, Mike Hailwood performed a now-legendary comeback at the Isle of Man TT in the Formula One race. Few believed the 38-year-old would be competitive after such a long absence, but such was the interest in his return that spectators were taking up positions seven hours before the race began. Riding a Ducati 900SS, he was not only competitive but won. It was his thirteenth TT victory and during the race he set six record-breaking laps in a fiercely contested battle with Phil Read.

He raced the following year at the Isle of Man. He rode a two-stroke Suzuki RG 500 to victory in the Senior TT, his fourteenth title. He then decided to use that same 500cc bike in the Unlimited Classic race and diced for the lead with Alex George riding an 1,100cc Honda for all six laps in yet another TT epic. Mike lost the race by just two seconds – so close to claiming a fifteenth TT title. Then, aged 39, he retired from racing for good.

In 1979 Mike Hailwood established a Honda-based retail motorcycle dealership in Birmingham named 'Hailwood and Gould', in partnership with another former motorcycle racer, Rodney Gould. But Mike was not destined for old age.

On Saturday, 21 March 1981, he set off in his Rover SD1 with his children, Michelle and David, to collect some fish and chips. As they returned along the A435 Alcester Road through Portway in Warwickshire, near their home in Tanworth-in-Arden, a heavy goods vehicle truck made an illegal turn through the barriers of the central reservation. Mike crashed into it. Michelle aged 9 was killed instantly. Mike and David were taken to hospital where Mike died two days later from severe internal injuries. David survived.

Mike Hailwood's motorcycle statistics put him in contention for being one of the greatest riders of all time. He retired with 76 Grand Prix victories, 10 world titles and 14 Isle of Man TT wins. In a 22-year bike racing career (1957-79) he rode in around 700 races and won over half of them.

He was awarded the Segrave Trophy for 1979 and received an MBE in recognition of his achievements and services to motorsport. The FIM named him a Grand Prix 'Legend' in the year 2000. In 1981 part of the Isle of Man TT course was named 'Hailwood's Height' in his honour. Hailwood and Purley share the distinction of risking their lives to save others and were rightly recognized for it.

Bibliography

Baxter, Raymond, *Tales of my Time*, Grub Street 2005

Davis, Anthony, *Woolf Barnato – Man About Town,* CreateSpace 2016

Davis, S.C.H., *My Life in Motorsport*, Herridge 2008

Evans, Art, *Ken Miles*, Enthusiast 2019

Foulkes, Nicholas, *The Bentley Era – The Fast & Furious Story of the Fabulous Bentley Boys,* Quadrille 2008

Posthumus, Cyril, *Sir Henry Segrave*, Batsford 1961

River, Charles (ed), *Eddie Rickenbacker – The Life & Legacy of America's Top World War I Fighter Ace*, CreateSpace 2017

Saward, Joe, *The Grand Prix Saboteurs*, Morienval 2006

Severn, Mark, *The Gambardier*, Leonaur 2007

Shelby, Carroll, *The Carroll Shelby Story,* Greymalkin 2020

Walker, Mick, *Mike Hailwood: The Fan's Favourite*, DB 2012

Walker, Murray, *Unless I'm Very Much Mistaken*, Harper Collins 2013

Williams, Richard, *Enzo Ferrari: A Life*, Yellow Jersey 2002

The National Archives

WO 372/23/41220 Medal Card for Muriel Thompson

ADM 196/122/36 Naval Record for George Pearson Glen Kidston

WO 95/3065/1 War Diary for 2/4 Battalion Royal Berkshire Regiment

WO 95/3065/1 Records 184 Infantry Brigade, 2 Battalion Royal Berkshire Regiment

WO 372/6/104489 Medal Card John Francis Duff

ADM 196/147/177 Naval Records George Pearson Glen Kidston

AIR 76/40/36 RAF/RFC records for Henry Ralph Stanley Birkin

WO 374 20981 Army Records for John Francis Duff

WO 339 65867 Army records for Bernard Rubin

WO 339 30592 Army records for Henry O'Neal de Hane Segrave

Journals and websites

Motorsport
FANY fany.org.uk Diary Extracts Muriel Thompson
The Brooklands Bulletin brooklandsmuseum.com
The Journal of the Brooklands Museum – Gwenda Hawkes
longlongtrail.co.uk
The First World War online archive for RGA general information & 244
    Siege Battery RGA
The National Army Museum nam.ac.uk

Images

Simon & Cath Kidston, images of Glen Kidston
Gail Woolston, images of David Purley

Index